Harvard Business Review

ON
STRATEGIC RENEWAL

THE HARVARD BUSINESS REVIEW PAPERBACK SERIES

The series is designed to bring today's managers and professionals the fundamental information they need to stay competitive in a fast-moving world. From the preeminent thinkers whose work has defined an entire field to the rising stars who will redefine the way we think about business, here are the leading minds and landmark ideas that have established the *Harvard Business Review* as required reading for ambitious businesspeople in organizations around the globe.

Other books in the series:

Other books in the series (continued):

Other books in the series (continued):

Harvard Business Review on the Mind of the Leader

Harvard Business Review on Motivating People

Harvard Business Review on Negotiation and Conflict Resolution

Harvard Business Review on Nonprofits

Harvard Business Review on Organizational Learning

Harvard Business Review on the Persuasive Leader

Harvard Business Review on Profiting from Green Business

Harvard Business Review on Strategic Alliances

Harvard Business Review on Strategic Sales Management

Harvard Business Review on Strategies for Growth

Harvard Business Review on Supply-Chain Management

Harvard Business Review on Talent Management

Harvard Business Review on Teams That Succeed

Harvard Business Review on the Tests of a Leader

Harvard Business Review on Top-Line Growth

Harvard Business Review on Turnarounds

Harvard Business Review on Women in Business

Harvard Business Review on Work and Life Balance

Harvard Business Review

ON

STRATEGIC RENEWAL

A HARVARD BUSINESS REVIEW PAPERBACK

The *Harvard Business Review* articles in this collection are available as individual reprints. Discounts apply to quantity purchases. For information and ordering, please contact Customer Service, Harvard Business School Publishing, Boston, MA 02163. Telephone: (617) 783-7500 or (800) 988-0886, 8 A.M. to 6 P.M. Eastern Time, Monday through Friday. Fax: (617) 783-7555, 24 hours a day. E-mail: custserv@hbsp.harvard.edu.

Library of Congress Cataloging-in-Publication Data
Harvard business review on strategic renewal.
        p.   cm. — (A Harvard business review paperback)
    Includes index.
    ISBN-978-1-4221-2648-6
    1. Strategic planning. 2. Organizational change.
3. Management. I. Harvard Business School Publishing Corporation.
II. Harvard business review.
HD30.28.H3795   2008
658.4'06—dc22   2008001135

Contents

Harvard Business Review

ON

STRATEGIC RENEWAL

Growth as a Process

An Interview with Jeffrey R. Immelt

THOMAS A. STEWART

Executive Summary

UNDER JACK WELCH'S LEADERSHIP, General Electric's managers applied their imaginations relentlessly to the task of making work more efficient. Jeffrey Immelt succeeded Welch as CEO on September 7, 2001, just in time to see the world change. Corporate scandals and terrorist attacks shook the global economy. In this fundamentally altered context, Immelt knew that GE could not simply cling to its status quo.

Harvard Business Review offers the first deep look under the hood of Immelt's GE. In conversation with editor Tom Stewart, Immelt was quick to point out that he is not leading a revolution; productivity is still important. But the new focus is on achieving organic revenue growth— and plenty of it. Immelt has set the audacious goal of increasing annual revenues from GE's existing businesses at two to three times the rate of global GDP growth.

Hitting that target will depend on deep cultural change and, in Immelt's words, "making it personal" for every one of his managers.

He's not afraid to pull the necessary levers. He has overseen changes to the company's famed talent management process (now, the highest-potential executives are the ones who exhibit "growth leadership traits"); established new performance metrics; invested in new marketing capabilities and R&D resources; and created new mechanisms to flag promising ideas. Immelt expects positive results from each of these moves, but the real payoff comes from combining them in a process design he calls "Execute for Growth." It's vital, he believes, to cast growth as a process because that allows him to tap into a traditional strength of the organization—its process orientation—and put it in the service of the new goal. Meanwhile, investors are reassured to the extent that GE's recent stellar organic growth seems like the reliable and repeatable output of a well-designed process.

When Jeff Immelt became chairman and CEO of General Electric, he took the helm of a fine-tuned productivity machine. GE had long taken management innovation seriously—from the company's famous blue book days in the 1950s to the development of its Crotonville training center into a management academy the equal of any on Earth. Under Jack Welch, GE's managers applied their imaginations relentlessly to the task of making work more efficient. Over a series of high-profile initiatives, Welch created a formidable tool kit and mind-set to maintain bottom-line discipline, while he fueled top-line growth largely through geographical expansion and acquisitions.

Immelt succeeded Welch in September of 2001, just in time to see the world change. Blows to the global economy came from corporate scandals and, more dramatically, from terrorist attacks on American soil. Operating in a fundamentally altered context, Immelt knew GE could not cling to its status quo.

Coming up on Jeff Immelt's fifth anniversary in office, Harvard Business Review offers the first deep look under the hood of Immelt's GE. In conversation with editor Tom Stewart, Immelt was quick to point out that he is not leading a revolution. Rather, the challenge has been "to take this great operating company and not lose anything, but add to it." The nature of the addition? A new and equally disciplined focus on organic growth.

Immelt put two of GE's traditional strengths—process orientation and the ability to develop, test, and deploy management ideas—in service of a different goal. That meant designing a process that could reliably draw new revenue streams from existing businesses. As with past initiatives, GE has not been secretive about the elements of the process; they were spelled out in its 2005 annual report and are presented here as an exhibit. That's because the payoff is not in the diagram but in the doing. All depends, in Immelt's words, on "making it personal" for individual managers.

Read on, and decide for yourself whether this process, under Immelt's leadership, will make the grade. The goal GE has set for sustained organic growth—two to three times the growth of global GDP—translates to about 8% today. Few companies have achieved the kind of growth GE is seeking, and none on a revenue base of $150 billion. In January, Immelt told GE's top managers at the annual meeting in Boca Raton, Florida, "The business book that can help you hasn't been written yet." For *him though, there's no other option. "Another decade of 4% growth, and GE will cease to be a great company," he said. "But if we can spur our growth rate without losing our productivity edge, GE will keep being the most admired company into the next century."*

You are determined to move GE from a culture of productivity to a culture of growth—organic growth, that is, and not growth by acquisition. Why?

We're now in a slow-growth world. Things were different 25 years ago. Oil was under $30 a barrel; most growth came from the developed world; we were a country at peace. After I came in as CEO, I looked at the world post-9/11 and realized that over the next ten or 20 years, there just was not going to be much tailwind. It would be a more global market, it would be more driven by innovation, and a premium would be placed on companies that could generate their own growth. We have to change the company—to become more innovation driven—in order to deal with this new environment. It's the right thing for investors. Productivity is still very important, but if you look back at GE's businesses over the past decade or so, those that have been managed for both productivity and growth have done the best.

For you, growth means sustaining an average organic revenue growth rate of about 8%, which nobody's ever done before. Why set that kind of goal?

Every initiative needs a metric. To find the right one, we studied about 30 companies. We looked at the percentage of sales attributable to products introduced in the past three years and maybe 15 other things like that. But when we brought those metrics back inside our culture, they didn't fit. They might work for other companies, but at GE, the only things that move the culture are ones that show up on our income statement. It's just the way we were raised. We finally came up with organic revenue growth as the only output function that goes straight into the ledger. We believe we can grow two to three times faster than world GDP. We made it in 2005, and we're going to make it in 2006. It's good to have aspirational goals in a company like GE.

How do the income statement and balance sheet for a company driven by organic growth look different from the financials for a company that grows mainly through productivity and acquisition?

Higher revenue, of course—and in our case, more of it global, because the market's more global. Lower general and administrative expense as a percentage of sales—I want that to go from 11% to 8% over the next four years. We'll have fewer rooftops, fewer divisions, more back-room outsourcing, and more common platforms and IT systems. We'll be cutting nongrowth costs as close to the bone as possible. But there will be more marketing expense and more R&D. We'll also see higher margins because we'll have a better flow of new products and, most important, services.

One thing that won't change is our capital efficiency. Philosophically, whether it's the productivity years or today, we like businesses like aircraft engines where we see probably $16 billion in revenue but capital expenditures of about $400 million. Capital efficiency like that generates a lot of cash.

The first big thing you did when you became CEO was throw a billion dollars into R&D. That was a fairly attention-getting growth bet.

I put a stake in the ground about products, innovation, and technology, because there we could lean into an existing infrastructure that was decent but needed to get out of the basement. This was an area where even small things would have an immediate impact. We put more than 100 million bucks into renovating our research center in upstate New York. We had already started a tech center in India, but we added new ones in China and Germany, and I made the businesses themselves spend more in R&D. And we started getting a flow of technology.

What was the rationale for the acquisitions you began making in 2003? How do they fit into an organic-growth objective?

We did a lot of heavy lifting in our portfolio because we didn't have enough juice. We saw where we needed to go, and we wouldn't get there with our existing businesses. So we bought homeland security, biotech, water—businesses that would give us a stronger foundation for innovation.

Around the same time, we started on the sales force and named Beth Comstock CMO to raise our game in marketing. By the end of 2003, we pulled together the best sales and marketing people in the company and formed the Commercial Council, which I chair. That turned out to be a big deal. The council was designed to share best practices and plan growth programs, but more fundamentally, it began to develop this idea of growth as a process.

*Why was that important? Why should organic growth
be cast as a process challenge?*

If you run a big multibusiness company like GE and
you're trying to lead transformative change, that objective has to be linked to hitting levers across all of the
businesses—and it must keep that up over time. So
you've got to have a process. That's true from an internal
standpoint, but it's also the only way you get paid in the
marketplace. Investors have to see that it's repeatable.

I knew if I could define a process and set the right
metrics, this company could go 100 miles an hour in
the right direction. It took time, though, to understand
growth as a process. If I had worked out that wheel-
shaped diagram in 2001, I would have started with it.
(See the exhibit "Execute for Growth: A Six-Part Process.") But in reality, you get these things by wallowing
in them awhile. We had a few steps worked out in 2003,
but it took another two years to fill in the process. Jack
was a great teacher in this regard. I would see him wal-
low in something like Six Sigma, where easily the first
two years were tough. People would say, "Whoa, what
the hell is this?" Still, he wouldn't move on to something else. He'd get the different businesses sharing
ideas, and everything always crystallized in the end. He
was a good initiative driver.

*What makes you think you won't continue to shape and
reshape the process?*

It reaches a point where you have to say, all right, this is
the framework. Organizations will tolerate iterating,
but they won't tolerate *permanent* iterating. I've got a
pretty good gut on when I'm making progress with the
company and when I'm frustrating people. If I'm at a

Manager Development Course, for example, doing a Q&A with employees, I might get up and start drawing the growth-as-a-process chart. While I'm doing that, I'm saying, "Guys, are you with me?" There's a look in their eyes that says, "OK, we get it," and then there's another look that says, "Not only do we get it—we don't want you to draw another circle. Let's keep it right there."

Execute for Growth: A Six-Part Process

General Electric's leaders use this diagram internally to explain how specific initiatives fit into a larger organic growth process.

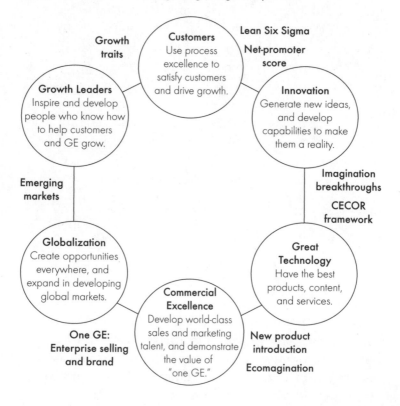

Growth traits

Customers
Use process excellence to satisfy customers and drive growth.

Lean Six Sigma

Net-promoter score

Growth Leaders
Inspire and develop people who know how to help customers and GE grow.

Innovation
Generate new ideas, and develop capabilities to make them a reality.

Emerging markets

Imagination breakthroughs

CECOR framework

Globalization
Create opportunities everywhere, and expand in developing global markets.

Commercial Excellence
Develop world-class sales and marketing talent, and demonstrate the value of "one GE."

Great Technology
Have the best products, content, and services.

One GE: Enterprise selling and brand

New product introduction

Ecomagination

So this is the process we've come up with. You can take each element apart and examine the components, and when you put them together again, they reinforce one another. If you're a leader at GE, you're going to hit on each of these elements several times a year. Every one of them has metrics, and every year you'll be pushed to drive the numbers higher. You can't escape it.

The diagram is a circle—there's no clear starting or ending point. But when you personally present it, you tend to begin with "great technology," which in some of your businesses translates to content leadership.

I start there instinctively. I'm not sure I have a scientific reason, but it may go back to my experience in appliances—I worked there for three years in the late 1980s—and to what I saw in the medical business. The thing is, you can be Six Sigma, you can do great delivery, you can be great in China, you can do everything else well—but if you don't have a good product, you're not going to sell much. That goes for turbines; it goes for TV; it goes for financial services. I told our company's top leaders at Boca, "If you can do only one thing well, this is what I'd pick: Make sure this pipeline is always full." The first thing I ask in a business review or a growth playbook [strategic-planning] session is how we stack up against our competitors from a product standpoint, given the customer's wants and needs. I make sure we fund for leadership. We've gotten out of businesses where funding for leadership couldn't get good results. Motors is an example. We couldn't see a way to get a good return even if we funded for leadership there, so we sold that business. Similarly, we used to have a private equity investment business. We shut that down because there was no product excellence. We were just a wallet.

Another element in the growth process is "commercial excellence"—putting great sales and marketing leadership in place, burnishing the brand, and so forth.

If we can create a sales and marketing function that's as good as finance at GE, I'll change this company. In a deflationary world, you could get margin by working productivity; now, you need marketing to get a price. Before we launched this growth initiative, marketing was the place where washed-up salespeople went. They were chart makers. We're talking about marketing as an aligned function again. We hired literally thousands of marketers. For the best of them, we created the Experienced Commercial Leadership Program, the kind of intensive course that we've long offered in audit and finance. That's 200 people a year, every year. We also resurrected the Advanced Marketing Management Seminar at Crotonville for senior executives. We put [Procter & Gamble's] A. G. Lafley on the board. We've been learning since we acquired Amersham in the health care business, because it's a lot closer to the pharmaceutical industry than our business was, and it's all about marketing. But it will take ten years to drive these changes. You don't just say, "I'm a marketing company" and become a marketing company.

Years ago, I was walking through a hotel lobby and saw a guy with a "Budgets Are for Wimps" coffee mug. When I commented on it, he told me his boss got one for everyone at their meeting. I said, "Are you guys in marketing?" And he said, "How did you guess?"

I've always worried about a jailbreak. How do we make sure people don't say, "Jeff doesn't care about productivity"? I think a lot about how to shine light on a new commercial leadership program and assure the audit staff that I still love them. I tell them, "Can you imagine how great this company is going to be if the salespeople are as good as you?" We're getting the sales force better trained and equipped with better tools and metrics. A good example is what we're doing to create discipline around pricing. Not long ago, a guy here named Dave McCalpin did an analysis of our pricing in appliances and found out that about $5 billion of it is discretionary. Given all the decisions that sales reps can make on their own, that's how much is in play. It was the most astounding number I'd ever heard—and that's just in appliances. Extrapolating across our businesses, there may be $50 billion that few people are tracking or accountable for. We would never allow something like that on the cost side. When it comes to the prices we pay, we study them, we map them, we work them. But with the prices we charge, we're too sloppy.

With stronger capabilities in place in sales and marketing, you can then start to connect the dots across the company. Isn't that the idea behind your push for more enterprise selling, where one salesperson can represent the company's entire range of offerings to a customer?

We've always done enterprise selling on an ad hoc basis, but we want to go beyond the convenient cross-selling opportunities and think more systematically about the kinds of customers that can benefit from our broad portfolio. If somebody's building a hospital, that might represent a total package of $1 billion, of which the GE market potential might be $100 million. We're probably already talking to the C-suite because we sell the medical equipment. What we need to do is set things up so that the medical rep can bring in the lighting rep, the turbine rep, and so on. The focus here is on four or five vertical industries and a couple of big events like the Olympics. Enterprise selling is only maybe 10% of the company's sales. But our market share is probably twice as high when we can combine things in that way.

Many companies are pursuing enterprise selling, and a common mistake seems to be that they try to do it to too many enterprises. How do you learn where to draw the line?

By failure. Tony Ecock in our health care business, who's been at it two and a half years, made a presentation at Boca on exactly this point. Our total enterprise contract value for 2004 and 2005 was $2.3 billion in health care. The mistake we made is we went to too many customers. The solution was better segmentation. By the way, Tony's analysis is now being shared through the Commercial Council, so we can do the same thing in energy and the other verticals.

Enterprise selling takes on other dimensions outside the country. When I go to China, I visit my contact at the National Development and Reform Commission, which is kind of China's department of energy, transportation, and health and human services. He'll pull out a little book and just start flipping the pages, saying, "In energy you're a little bit high; Siemens is the low bid. You might want to correct that. On the rail program, you look pretty good. Health care, you had a good year. . . ." He's connecting the dots for us. In Qatar, the emir wants to know everybody doing business in his country. In a dinner set up to talk about oil and gas bids, he might say, "Jeff, I'm going to put $10 billion into a hospital," or he might mention that they're going to buy GE engines for Qatar Airways. India, on the other hand, is very commercial, so you're not going to deal company-to-country there. You've got to knock on a lot of different doors. Mahindra & Mahindra might buy differently from Tata, and Reliance Energy, being private, is going to buy differently from the national utility.

How does a cross-business, high-visibility campaign like "ecomagination" fit into the idea of commercial excellence?

Ecomagination is an integrated marketing campaign, connecting the dots from a marketing standpoint in the way that enterprise selling connects the dots from a sales standpoint. The goal was to strengthen the company by picking a theme that was bigger than just energy, or rail, or aircraft engines, or plastics. We'd never done anything like that before. But in 2004, it came up in our strategic-planning process, S-1, that there was a big theme emerging across five different businesses—a real focus on emissions reduction, energy efficiency, water supply, and what I would call generally the economics of scarcity.

The very economics, by the way, that drove you to read the demand for organic growth. You're trying to make tailwind out of the headwind.

Exactly right. So we plugged that input from S-1 into the Commercial Council, which studied it for nine months. We met with people from NGOs, government offices, and other relevant organizations. We brought a lot of assets together, including our knowledge of public policy and how it gets influenced. Once we had done our homework, we launched ecomagination with 17 products we could point to. As always, we were metric driven. We said that our $10 billion of revenue from products tapping renewable energy sources like the sun and wind had to go to $20 billion in five years. The $750 million we were spending on R&D for clean technologies had to go to a billion and a half. Our own greenhouse gas emissions had to come down by 1% by 2012.

Has there been any push back from your customers, some of whom I can imagine would rather stick to their carbon-burning ways?

There were plenty of guys on our energy team who hated this in the beginning because half of their customers were saying *they* hated it. Never mind that half of the customers loved it. We just kept talking: "Here's where we're going. Here's why we think it's good for both of us. And it's going to come someday anyhow, so let's get ahead of it." We hosted what we call a dreaming session in the summer of 2004 with the 30 biggest utilities. Some of the top players in the industry—CEOs like Jim Rogers and David Rutledge—came to Crotonville and heard Jeff Sachs from Columbia talk about global warming. There were other speakers who were pretty compelling on different topics, and breakout sessions. I floated the idea of doing something on public policy on greenhouse gases, and we had a good debate.

In part, ecomagination helped to show the organization that we can do these things. The company has been great in terms of management practice but more reluctant when it comes to what I would call business innovation. Ecomagination was one way to show the organization that it's OK to stick your neck out and even to make customers a little bit uncomfortable.

Let's move on to globalization, another part of your growth process. I'm struck by something I've heard your executives say—that developing a product for Malaysia or India can't happen through "defeaturization." The right solution is not an American product stripped down to meet an Indian price, but a truly Indian product designed from the ground up to carry an Indian price.

It's a big change in orientation, and we talk a lot about it—but to be candid, it's still mostly aspirational. This year we put together a team of 25 people from across the company to figure out what it takes to go from a defeaturing mind-set to a customer optimization mind-set. When we have our growth playbook session (our old S-1 process) this summer, that is going to be a prominent part of it. So when Dave Calhoun, for example, gets up to talk about the infrastructure business, he's going to have to say, "Here's what I have to do in infrastructure to have more developing-market interplay." Maybe for aircraft engines it won't be much, but in energy or water, it's going to be a big deal. We're putting 50 people on the ground in India to help with the "1 lakh car" [a vehicle that will cost customers 100,000 rupees, or roughly $2,250] that Ratan Tata is behind. The assumption is that it will be made of plastic, so it could mean a lot to our plastics business. This may be my hottest topic right now. We can't develop CT scanners in Milwaukee for China; we've got to develop them in China.

And if the Chinese customer is different from the Indian customer, is different from the North American customer—

So be it.

What makes local product development so hard? Or, to look at it another way, what do you think the components of the solution are?

There are at least three pieces. It's different people. It's funding differently—taking money out of the United States and western Europe and allowing people to spend it in their own regions so that they can really optimize it. And it's about being better at adaptable and low-cost manufacturing. So, coming out of this study, we'll make some decisions on people and where they go, we'll change some funding, and then, as part of our growth playbook, we want to come up with ten emerging-market products. We want to do a $500,000 MRI machine that is a step function different from anything we've ever made. We also want to make a village-level desalination product. Right now, if you're Algeria and you're going to drop $2 billion into the most sophisticated desalination plant in the world, we've got that covered. What we don't have is a $35,000 municipal water system that can be deployed easily. Investors who don't know the reality of the developing world see this kind of thinking and say, "God, this is risky." And I say, "You want to see something risky, try selling a lightbulb to a big-box retailer." I think we can get a 45% to 50% contribution margin on a product like this if we design it there, if we make it there, and if it never gets touched by someone in Milwaukee or someplace far away like that. It needs to leverage global technology, but it's got to be in the market and of the market.

GE has been aggressively globalizing its talent base, but it seems as if you are looking for something deeper than a diversity of faces. You want to make it credible that any boy or girl growing up anywhere in the world could end up in the office you hold—and that the full spectrum of career development can start anywhere in GE.

That is absolutely what we want to see. That's why we went straight to the audit staff, straight into the heartbeat of the company. There are about 400 young people on the audit staff, and maybe 60 are Indian. Our CFO, Keith Sherin, has said that in the next year, we're going to have 185 FMP participants in Asia (FMP is the two-year financial management program we use to launch GE management careers). Eventually, that group will funnel down to about 60 we can put on the audit staff. Again, we can't snap our fingers to make the change, but in a four-year time period, we can move the needle in a pretty substantial way.

Meanwhile, you've identified a new set of growth traits for all of GE's leaders.

There are so many great traits in this organization that I never want to lose. People are friendly, competitive, hardworking. What I've always loved about GE is it's a working person's company. But we knew that we wouldn't be growth oriented without some change to our DNA. So we benchmarked 15 companies that had grown organically for a decade at three times the GDP—Dell and Toyota, for instance, and some of our own businesses, like consumer finance. We looked at who their people were and what they did. By the end of 2004, we came up with five growth traits. The first is external focus. Then there's imagination and creativity. And a growth leader must be especially decisive and capable of clear thinking. Inclusiveness is also vital. Finally, leaders in these high-growth companies tend to have deep domain expertise.

We came up with a tool that we'll use as part of Session C, our annual HR review. It's a matrix that lists the five growth traits and their components. You're rated as green, yellow, or red on each one. Everybody has to have one red because the point is not to pick out winners and losers—it's to say everybody's got to work on something. That will guide the development plans for the top 5,000 people in the company this year.

What's red for you? Where do you think you could use the most work?

Decisiveness. At my level in the company, it's clearly the thing that moves the needle the most. One of the things I've learned by experience is that you can run a productivity company and not have to give a lot of straight yes or no answers. You can make your base costs by cutting everybody by 10%, and you can do OK for a long time that way. But you can't drive a growth company by cutting everybody by 10%—or by adding 10%. You have to make higher-level moves, and that takes clear decision making.

How do you take these traits and turn them into the machine that produces the talent you need?

What we'll get from this year's Session C will be diagnostic. We might see that the consumer finance business is all red in one area and all green in another. Then we'll decide how its training should change, and so on. This is the strength of the GE model. If you think about it, I own all the means of correction. I can send people who have a gap to school, and then I've got the audit staff to make sure they go.

The focus on organic growth is also going to require people to stay in the same jobs longer. You can't plant a tree and see it grow in a year. This is very countercultural in an organization where building a career has always meant packing your bags every 18 months. Going forward, you're still going to have some 18-month jobs, but over the course of 30 years, you're going to have more jobs that last five years.

Besides saner home lives, the benefit of keeping people in position longer is what?

Deeper domain knowledge. If you dispel the myths of our company, which is what I have to do sometimes, you see that the most successful parts of GE are places where leaders have stayed in place a long time. Think of Brian Rowe's long tenure in aircraft engines. Four or five big decisions he made—relying on his deep knowledge of that business—won us maybe as many as 50 years of industry leadership. The same point applies to GE Capital. The places where we've churned people, like reinsurance, are where you will find we've failed.

At the same time that you're urging your people to become more externally focused, you're also talking about externalizing GE's legendary internal process excellence. Can you explain that part of the growth process?

This was an idea that began with benchmarking Toyota. People there impressed upon us that Toyota is a very process-driven company and the purpose of that is to delight customers and annihilate competitors. Now, GE is certainly a process-driven company. But I would say that if you interviewed GE employees and asked why we did Six Sigma, you wouldn't get that answer. We decided that somehow we had to take some of our processes and embed them into how we beat the competition and how we delight customers.

We started with two things. First, lean processes. We realized that the notion of reducing cycle time and waste was a great fit with the challenges of interacting with customers. We applied it to things like bringing down the time needed to install an MRI machine. That used to take 65 days. Now it takes 15.

Second, we created an offering called "At the Customer, for the Customer," which involves doing Six Sigma projects in GE customers' operations to help them be more successful. We're doing this, for example, with a big health systems company where we're embedding a dozen people—we call them "performance solutions"—who will train the company's employees on Six Sigma and work with them to apply it to the billing process, the emergency room, any six areas the company chooses.

You're now using some new measurements to gauge your success with customers.

When we run our business management courses, we ask people to work on real problems we're trying to solve. In 2004, we sent one class out to study companies with the reputation of being best in class. One of the things that group discovered is you've got to have a customer satisfaction metric, and that is doubly true for GE, since nothing happens in this company without an output metric.

Our first response, in 2005, was to have each business adopt one operating and one social metric for customer satisfaction. The social metric we liked the best was the thing you published by Fred Reichheld—the net-promoter score, or the percentage of people who say they would recommend GE to a friend, minus those who wouldn't. (See "The One Number You Need to Grow," HBR December 2003.) So we standardized that across all the businesses. Now aviation, for example, has a net-promoter score and the operating metric that makes the most sense for that business: time on wing. It's useful to have at least one score standard across the company, because that way we can spread learning.

That brings us around to "imagination breakthroughs" on the chart. Those seem to be a way of injecting energy into the system.

If you want to have growth, you've got to make sure that there are tough projects being done and you shine a light on them. We created imagination breakthroughs to pull some ideas out of the pile that we thought were really hard or really important and could possibly generate $100 million in new sales over a three-year horizon. Imagination breakthroughs are a protected class of ideas—safe from the budget slashers because I've blessed each one. They help make organic growth real to the company and to the Street. At this point, there are about 100 of them, half involving brand-new products and half involving changing commercial structure. Ultimately, I'd like to see the concept morph and spread into the organization so that we have 1,000 imagination breakthroughs and the focus is less on these big elephants and more on creativity throughout the businesses.

An example of an imagination breakthrough project is the hybrid locomotive. It's got a program manager who's been selected by me, it's funded, and every best practice we know of in the company is going to be applied to it. I'm going to look at it once a month, in terms of status, and see to it that what is being learned in the project is disseminated. What we're trying to do with imagination breakthroughs is take risks, using my point of view.

Do you mean that the CEO's point of view on a project like this would be different from, say, a business unit head's point of view? Why would that be true?

I have the biggest risk profile and the broadest time horizon in the company. So looking at the evolution of the hybrid locomotive, we're talking about tens of millions of dollars. For the program manager, it's huge, the most massive thing he's ever managed. For John Dineen, who runs the rail business, it's pretty big. For me, you know, it's OK. We can do it. The program manager wants it to get done tomorrow. John Dineen says, "Jeez, I may be in this job four, five years." But I'll probably be here much longer. I'll see the hybrid locomotive—I absolutely know that. So I can bring to bear the right risk-taking and time horizon trade-offs.

I review about eight imagination breakthroughs every month and have all eight program managers sitting around the table. Behind each one is an actual picture of what that person's working on, a desalination plant or new Monogram refrigerator or GE engine, to help keep it real. I don't want to see any long-winded PowerPoint presentations. I just have a little profile of each program in front of me, and I want the program managers to talk to me. I ask, "What is the biggest internal barrier? What is the biggest external barrier? Are you on time? What's the revenue flow?"

The other day, we had three people from financial services, one person from health care, one from rail, and a few focused on distribution channels. One person was presenting on Internet credit card applications. "My biggest bottleneck," she said, "is I don't have the right kind of IT search engine that can do all my credit approval, so I'm using sneakerware. It's hurting my growth." So I asked the team, "What's it going to take to have the same capability that Citigroup or American Express has?" And we had a real debate about how to get this done.

At a meeting last year, reviewing the value products for health care with Joe Hogan, who runs the business, we added $20 million in funding and took the responsibility for the value products away from the product lines and put it in China. That was how we removed an internal barrier: The mother business was squeezing it. In the year since, sales have gone from $60 million to $260 million. At a recent update for those same products, we talked more about an external barrier: how we might design knockdown kits so that we could design the thing and make a kit in India but have it assembled in China and avoid the tariffs and duties. Those are the discussions you want to have there.

It sounds like an intense experience for the program managers.

One of the things this process has taught us is we don't have enough sophisticated product managers and great systems engineers to put in charge of high-visibility programs like these. If there's a $100 million investment project, we might, out of the 310,000 people in the company, have 30 who really know how to spend that amount of money effectively. That's probably not enough. It has presented an organizational weakness, and at Session C this year, we're going to home in on building that capability.

The imagination breakthrough part of the growth process seems the most counter to the productivity culture that dominated when you came here. How do you make sure people get it?

I'm a translator. Every CEO has to be. When we have an idea factory like IDEO talk to us about innovation, it's my job to translate what they say into GE. That means putting it in terms of process and metrics.

OK, take IDEO's idea of rapid prototyping. They say, "Have a beginner's mind," and "Prototype in a day." Translate that into GE.

That's risk mitigation for imagination breakthroughs. I'm serious. What I'm saying is, don't think about this as brainstorming; think about it as a way to measure risk, understand failure rates, and learn what customers think, so we can run through more ideas without increasing the overall amount of risk.

GE's 2004 annual report sounded a self-assured note. You titled it—and by extension, the current era—"Our Time." What were you signaling?

Only what I remind myself of every day—that achieving this kind of growth depends on making it the personal mission of everyone here. If we want, we can cloak our-selves in the myth of the professional manager and hide any problem in a process flowchart. But if I want people to take more risks, solve bigger problems, and grow the business in a way that's never been done before, I have to make it personal. So I tell people, "Start your career tomorrow. If you had a bad year, learn from it and do better. If you had a good year, I've already forgotten about it."

This is not a place for small-timers. Working at GE is the art of thinking and playing big; our managers have to work cross function, cross region, cross company. And we have to be about big purposes. We *can* solve health care. I like to remind people, if you fail here—well, what will happen? You'll leave and get a bigger job somewhere else. But if you win here, what's behind door number two? You get to be in the front seat of history, creating the future.

The Productivity Tool Kit

WHEN JEFF IMMELT BECAME GE's chairman and CEO in 2001, the organization already had a robust tool kit in place to tackle business problems. Most of its key initia-tives have focused on enhancing productivity.

- *Best Practices Sharing:* identifies particularly effective approaches and spreads them across GE's businesses
- *Change Acceleration Process:* equips leaders with a proven method of managing change and prepares them to succeed as change agents

- **Crotonville Customer Programs:** deploy the resources of GE's renowned internal training facility for the benefit of customers

- **Multigenerational Product Development Plan:** ensures that new products are not simply optimized for the near term but have the ability to evolve with customer needs

- **Process Mapping:** creates visual representations of business processes to facilitate understanding and simplification

- **Quick Market Intelligence:** builds on Wal-Mart's innovation of tapping into real-time data about customer and competitor behavior and disseminating that insight rapidly throughout the organization

- **Simplification:** drives out extraneous costs incurred by overcomplicated processes and proliferation of options in sourcing and other areas

- **Six Sigma:** employs Motorola-pioneered methods to bring defect levels below 3.4 defects per million opportunities. Intensive quality training yields "green belts," "black belts," and "master black belts"

- **Work-Out:** uses cross-functional teams and town hall meetings to find ways to take unproductive work out of the system, like meetings, reports, and approval levels that add no value

---

The Growth Tool Kit

A NEW SET OF TOOLS has been added to the old kit to help GE achieve its goals for top-line growth.

- *Acquisition Integration Framework:* outlines a detailed process for ensuring that acquired entities are effectively assimilated into GE

- *At the Customer, for the Customer:* brings GE's internal best practices, management tools, and training programs to customers facing their own managerial challenges

- **CECOR Marketing Framework:** connects innovation and other growth efforts with market opportunities and customer needs by asking questions to *calibrate, explore, create, organize,* and *realize* strategic growth

- *Customer Dreaming Sessions:* assemble a group of the most influential and creative people in an industry to envision its future and provoke the kind of interchange that can inspire new plans

- *Growth Traits and Assessments:* outline and enforce the expectation that GE's next generation of leaders will display five strengths: external focus, clear thinking, imagination, inclusiveness, and domain expertise

- *Imagination Breakthroughs:* focus top management's attention and resources on promising ideas for new revenue streams percolating up from anywhere in the organization

- *Innovation Fundamentals:* equip managers with four exercises to engage people in innovation, and prepare them to transform new ideas into action

- *Innovation Labs and Tool Kit:* support business strategy, product development, and other cross-functional project teams with a variety of resources and materials relevant to innovation efforts

- *Lean Showcases:* demonstrate the power of "lean" thinking by allowing people to see how cycle times were reduced in a core customer-facing business process

- **Lean Six Sigma:** puts the Six Sigma methods and tools in the service of a critical goal—reducing cycle times in the processes that chiefly drive customer satisfaction

- **Net-Promoter Score:** holds all GE businesses to a new standard: They must track and improve the percentage of customers who would recommend GE. The scores are seen as leading indicators of growth performance; business teams apply lean Six Sigma and other tools to analyze scores and identify and implement improvements.

Originally published in June 2006
Reprint R0606C

The Institutional Yes

An Interview with Jeff Bezos

JULIA KIRBY AND THOMAS A. STEWART

Executive Summary

SINCE ITS FOUNDING, in 1995, Amazon.com's bold moves have often left observers scratching their heads, if not predicting the company's demise. Why open up an effective proprietary retail platform to competition from third-party sellers? Why make tools that Amazon developed for its own use available to other website developers? (Why, for that matter, post negative reviews of your products?) Two HBR editors interviewed Bezos, the founder and CEO, to learn what's different about strategy formulation at Amazon. They came away with the sense that the company's strategy and culture are rooted in a sturdy entrepreneurial optimism and rest on the single question of what's better for the customer.

Bezos describes himself as "congenitally customer focused." He knows that the buyers in Amazon's consumer-facing business want selection, low prices, and fast delivery—and he's confident that won't change. "I can't imagine," he says, "that ten years from now [our customers] are going to say, 'I love Amazon, but if only they could deliver my products a little more slowly.'"

Competitor-focused companies risk complacency when they become industry leaders, he maintains, but customer-focused companies must always keep improving. "Years from now," Bezos says, "when people look back at Amazon, I want them to say that we uplifted customer-centricity across the entire business world."

If Amazon has made strategic mistakes, he says, they have been errors of omission. So when something seems like an opportunity, Bezos asks the question, "Why not?" which leads to maximizing the number of experiments companywide: "People say, 'We're going to do this. We're going to figure out a way.'" That's the institutional yes.

Amazon.com was born of strategy. The story has often been told of how founder Jeff Bezos, working in a quantitative analysis group at an investment firm, spotted an opportunity to sell books on the Internet. No native of the book-selling industry, he arrived at his business model logically: Given the attributes of the product and the structure of the supply chain, a no-bricks retailer could clearly make it—and make it big. Since its founding, in 1995, Amazon has continued to show a knack for spotting white spaces and a willingness to jump into them, even as it works to make spaces it already occupies more productive. The company's latest bold move is its "developer-facing" business: a set of offerings that make tools Amazon developed for its own use available to other website developers. Like so many other Amazon ventures, this one is based on sound logic—yet it's surprising. It's not the kind of thing one sees many companies doing.

Enough of these moves have paid off that HBR decided to look into what's different about strategy formulation at Amazon. How do ideas come under consideration, and how are commitments made? Is it a matter of one ingredient—Jeff Bezos—or is it an institutional capability? Thomas A. Stewart, HBR's editor in chief, and Julia Kirby, a senior editor, met with Bezos on two occasions to learn more. The conversations were wide-ranging and lively, punctuated frequently by Bezos's famous laugh. (He says that his wife, MacKenzie, often tells people, "If Jeff is unhappy, wait five minutes.") They came away with a sense that Amazon's strategy and culture are rooted in a sturdy entrepreneurial optimism. The following is an edited presentation of those talks.

Who is setting strategic direction for Amazon? At the very beginning it was just you, sitting in a car on the way from New York to Seattle, making all the plans. Are you still making them all?

Oh, heavens, no. We have a group called the S Team—S meaning "senior"—that stays abreast of what the company is working on and delves into strategy issues. It meets for about four hours every Tuesday. Once or twice a year the S Team also gets together in a two-day meeting where different ideas are explored. Homework is assigned ahead of time. A lot of the things discussed in those meetings are not that urgent—we're a few years out and can really think and talk about them at length. Eventually we have to choose just a couple of things, if they're big, and make bets.

The key is to ensure that this happens fractally, too, not just at the top. The guy who leads Fulfillment by Amazon, which is the web service we provide to let people use our fulfillment center network as a big computer peripheral, is making sure the strategic thinking happens for that business in a similar way. At different scale levels it's happening everywhere in the company. And the most important thing is that all of it is informed by a cultural point of view. There's a great Alan Kay quote: "Perspective is worth 80 IQ points." Some of our strategic capability comes from that.

How would you describe that cultural point of view?

First, we are willing to plant seeds and wait a long time for them to turn into trees. I'm very proud of this piece of our culture, because I think it is somewhat rare. We're not always asking ourselves what's going to happen in the next quarter, and focusing on optics, and doing those other things that make it very difficult for some publicly traded companies to have the right strategy.

Do you know when you're planting one of those seeds that it's, say, an acorn and it's going to turn into an oak? Do you have a strong vision of how things will materialize? Or does the shape emerge along the way?

We may not know that it's going to turn into an *oak*, but at least we know that it can turn out to be that big. I think you need to make sure with the things you choose that you are able to say, "If we can get this to work, it will be big." An important question to ask is, "Is it big enough to be meaningful to the company as a whole if we're very successful?"

Every new business we've ever engaged in has initially been seen as a distraction by people externally, and sometimes even internally. They'll say, "Why are you expanding outside of media products? Why are you going international? Why are you entering the market-place business with third-party sellers?" We're getting it now with our new infrastructure web services: "Why take on this new set of developer customers?" These are fair questions. There's nothing wrong with asking them. But they all have at their heart one of the reasons that it's so difficult for incumbent companies to pursue new initiatives. It's because even if they are wild successes, they have no meaningful impact on the company's economics for years. What I have found—and this is an empirical observation; I see no reason why it *should* be the case, but it tends to be—is that when we plant a seed, it tends to take five to seven years before it has a meaningful impact on the economics of the company.

That does require people, inside and outside, to keep the faith. How do you have the confidence that the investment will ultimately pay off?

It helps to base your strategy on things that won't change. When I'm talking with people outside the company, there's a question that comes up very commonly: "What's going to change in the next five to ten years?" But I very rarely get asked "What's *not* going to change in the next five to ten years?" At Amazon we're always trying to figure that out, because you can really spin up flywheels around those things. All the energy you invest in them today will still be paying you dividends ten years from now. Whereas if you base your strategy first and foremost on more transitory things—who your competitors are, what kind of technologies are available, and so on—those things are going to change so rapidly that you're going to have to change your strategy very rapidly, too.

What are some of the things you're counting on not to change?

For our business, most of them turn out to be customer insights. Look at what's important to the customers in our consumer-facing business. They want selection, low prices, and fast delivery. This can be different from business to business: There are companies serving other customers who wouldn't put price, for example, in that set. But having found out what those things are for our customers, I can't imagine that ten years from now they are going to say, "I love Amazon, but if only they could deliver my products a little more slowly." And they're not going to, ten years from now, say, "I really love Amazon, but I wish their prices were a little higher." So we know that when we put energy into defect reduction, which reduces our cost structure and thereby allows lower prices, that will be paying us dividends ten years from now. If we keep putting energy into that flywheel, ten years from now it'll be spinning faster and faster.

Another thing that we believe is pretty fundamental is that the world is getting increasingly transparent—that information perfection is on the rise. If you believe that, it becomes strategically smart to align yourself with the customer. You think about marketing differently. If in the old world you devoted 30% of your attention to building a great service and 70% of your attention to shouting about it, in the new world that inverts. A lot of our strategy comes from having very deep points of view about things like this, believing that they are going to be stable over time, and making sure our activities line up with them. Of course there could also come a day when one of those things turns out to be wrong. So it's important to have some kind of mechanism to figure out if you're wrong about a deeply held precept.

You've got two other sets of customers: the third parties who are selling goods through your site and this new set—the developers who can benefit from the tools you've created over the years. What are some constants for those groups?

We're still working on identifying them for the developer community, although we have some good guesses as to what they are. Reliability of the platform would be one, which is kind of a no-brainer. But then a lot of these things are no-brainers. No-brainers are no-brainers for a reason: They actually are important. As for the sellers, the number one thing that sellers want is sales.

Is that why the auction business didn't work out for Amazon—because eBay already had a lock on the sales those sellers wanted?

Actually, no, it's a little different from that. It's that our customers who are buyers are very convenience motivated. We make it really, really easy to buy things. You can see that if you look at a metric like our revenue per click or revenue per page turn. It's very high, because we're efficient for people. If you're a customer who wants

Amazon's Course

The company opened for business on the World Wide Web in July 1995, offering an unprecedented selection of books and 24/7 shopping every day of the year. Since then its constant tweaking of the buying experience, steady addition of new product categories, and periodic bold ventures have fueled dramatic revenue growth.

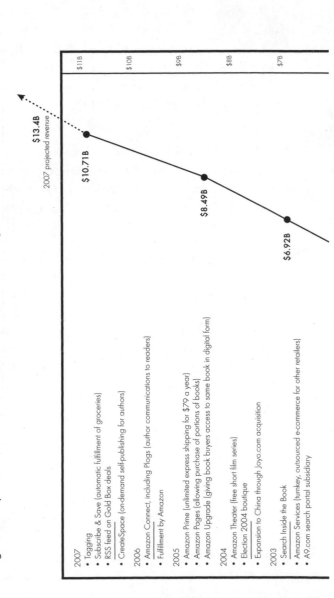

2007
- Tagging
- Subscribe & Save (automatic fulfillment of groceries)
- RSS feed on Gold Box deals
- CreateSpace (on-demand self-publishing for authors)

2006
- Amazon Connect, including Plogs (author communications to readers)
- Fulfillment by Amazon

2005
- Amazon Prime (unlimited express shipping for $79 a year)
- Amazon Pages (allowing purchase of portions of books)
- Amazon Upgrade (giving book buyers access to same book in digital form)

2004
- Amazon Theater (free short film series)
- Election 2004 boutique
- Expansion to China through Joyo.com acquisition

2003
- Search Inside the Book
- Amazon Services (turnkey, outsourced e-commerce for other retailers)
- A9.com search portal subsidiary

$13.4B
2007 projected revenue

$10.71B

$8.49B

$6.92B

$11B

$10B

$9B

$8B

$7B

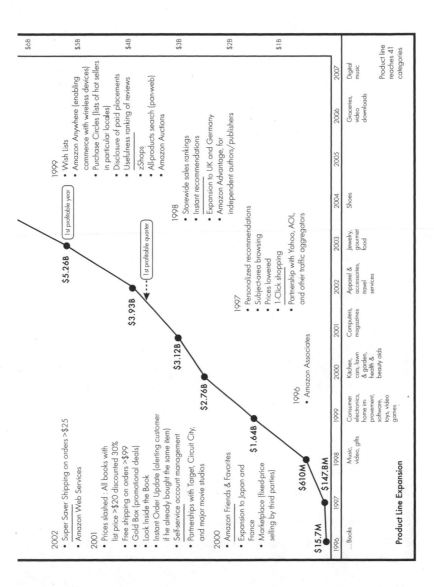

that kind of quick service, you do not want to wait till an auction closes. An auction is more about playing a game. There's some fun involved. You're not necessarily just trying to get the job done. It's a different kind of thing and a different customer segment.

That episode is actually one of the highlights of our corporate history—one that I tell over and over internally, because it speaks to persistence and relentlessness. The basic thought was: Look, we have this website where we sell things, and we want to have vast selection. One of the ways to get vast selection is to invite other sellers, third parties, onto our website to participate alongside us, and make it into a win-win situation. So we did auctions, but we didn't like the results. Next we created zShops, which was fixed-price selling but still parked those third parties in separate parts of the store. If a third-party seller had a used copy of *Harry Potter* to sell, it would have its own detail page, rather than having its availability listed right next to the new book. We still didn't like the results we got. It was when we went to the single-detail-page model that our third-party business really took off. Now, if we're offering a certain digital camera and you're a seller with the same camera to sell, you can go right on our own detail page, right next to our product, and underbid us. And if you do, we will put you in the "buy" box, which is on that page.

That can't have been an easy decision—it gets you the seller customer but loses you the buyer customer, doesn't it?

It was a very controversial decision internally at the time. Imagine being our digital camera buyer and you've just bought 10,000 units of a particular digital camera. Your boss says to you, "Good news: You know all those people you've been thinking of as your competitors? We're going to invite them to put their digital cameras right next to yours on your detail page." The natural reaction is "*What?*" A digital camera today is like a fish in a super-market. It's aging fast. You don't want to get stuck with a huge inventory of five-megapixel cameras when cus-tomers will shortly want six-megapixel cameras. You'll have to sell them for pennies on the dollar. So our buyers were extremely concerned—and rightly. They were say-ing, "Let me just make sure I understand this. I might get stuck with inventory of 10,000 units of this camera that I just loaded up on, and you're going to let just anybody come in and take Amazon traffic on what is our primary retail real estate, which is the detail page, and I'm going to lose the buy box to this other person because they have a lower price than me?" And we said, "Yeah, we are."

We talked about that a lot before we did it. But when the intellectual conversation gets too hard because of these potential cannibalization issues, we take a simple-minded approach. There's an old Warren Buffett story, that he has three boxes on his desk: in-box, out-box, and too hard. Whenever we're facing one of those too-hard problems, where we get into an infinite loop and can't decide what to do, we try to convert it into a straight-forward problem by saying, "Well, what's better for the consumer?"

The reality is that we have a highly competitive cost structure and we're very good at competing on things like digital cameras on that page, so it actually works out very well. But some of the most important things we've done over the years have been short-term tactical losers. In the very earliest days (I'm taking you back to 1995), when we started posting customer reviews, a customer might trash a book and the publisher wouldn't like it. I would get letters from publishers saying, "Why do you allow negative reviews on your website? Why don't you just show the positive reviews?" One letter in particular said, "Maybe you don't understand your business. You make money when you *sell* things." But I thought to myself, We don't make money when we sell things; we make money when we help customers make purchase decisions.

So you're choosing projects based on stable customer needs and adopting the customer's perspective to make difficult strategic decisions. Michael Porter claims that strategy is shaped by five forces, but we're hearing you talk about only one.

I think somehow I am congenitally customer focused. And I think that from that comes this passion to figure out customer-focused strategies as opposed to, say, competitor-focused strategies. There's nothing wrong with competitor focus. There are other companies that have delivered exceedingly good business results by pursuing close-follower strategies, setting up really good benchmarking tools. There's a lot to be said for that kind of passion. It doesn't happen to be who we are. We don't ignore our competitors; we try to stay alert to what they are doing, and certainly there are things that we benchmark very carefully. But a lot of our energy and drive as a company, as a culture, comes from trying to build these customer-focused strategies. And actually I do think they work better in fast-changing environments, for two reasons. First, as I said before, customer needs change more slowly—assuming you pick the right ones—than a lot of other things. Second, close following doesn't work as well in a fast-changing environment. The strategic value of close following is in not having to go down all the blind alleys. You let smaller competitors check those out, and when they find something good, you just quadruple down. If you're following close enough, and the arena is slow-moving enough, the fact that you're not first down that path doesn't hurt you much. But in our environment there's so much rapid change on the Internet, in technology, that our customer-obsessed approach is very effective.

There's another situation, too, where I think being customer focused is better, and that's when you're a leader. If you're competitor focused, you tend to slack off when your benchmarks say that you're the best. But if your focus is on customers, you keep improving. So there are a lot of advantages. I'm not claiming we invented this approach—a lot of companies are customer focused— but it's very deeply ingrained in all the nooks and crannies of our culture.

It could be that you have been able to take it to a new level. Being the instantiation of that model at the moment when it became possible to get a flood of customer feedback was happy timing.

It's totally true. We have the opportunity for Amazon not just to be a customer-centric company but to set a new standard globally for what "customer-centric" means. After World War II, Morita-san [Akio Morita, Sony's longtime leader] set a goal for Sony. He wanted the company to be known for quality, but his bigger goal for Sony was to make Japan known for quality. Having that kind of bigger mission is very inspiring. Years from now, when people look back at Amazon, I want them to say that we uplifted customer-centricity across the entire business world. If we can do that, it will be really cool.

In many companies it's hard to keep that customer focus. As the enterprise itself grows, internal agendas start to drive decisions. How do you defend against that? Are you constantly broadcasting the points of view that you hope will deeply inform the culture?

We have three all-hands meetings a year, so that's one mechanism for it. And then, repetition-wise, we've been saying the same things for many years. I constantly talk about things like information perfection and customer obsession relative to competitor obsession. We also do a bunch of things to keep people directly in touch with customer needs. Every new employee, no matter how senior or junior, has to go spend time in our fulfillment centers within the first year of employment. Every two years they do two days of customer service. Everyone has to be able to work in a call center.

Even you?

Oh, yeah. I just got recertified about six months ago. The fact that I did a lot of customer service in the first two years has not exempted me. Besides, it's quite entertaining, and you learn a ton. It's not a chore.

These mechanical things continually add fuel to that preexisting fire, but the truth is that corporate cultures are incredibly stable over time. They are self-perpetuating, because they attract new people who like that kind of culture, while the people who don't like it eject themselves. One of the things I hear most from new executives, once they've been here for a month, is

"I can't believe how customer focused this place is." So if you were someone who really loved a competitor-obsessed company and you came to Amazon, one of two things would happen. Either you would see our approach and say, "Wow, this is actually pretty cool; my eyes have been opened," or you would say, "This isn't for me." You might not use the word "culture," but you'd be missing something. So there's a very strong self-reinforcing loop. That is why cultures are very hard for competitors to copy—and a source of great competitive advantage if you have the right culture for the right mission. They also limit. There are things that you cannot undertake. You have to be accepting of what your culture is in your thinking about strategy.

That would mean the culture of a company is very path dependent. With the first few people you hire and your first few experiences, things start down a path.

They absolutely do. I'll tell you a story about an incident that I'm sure is part of the reason we are what we are. Sometime around May of 1997 we were put on a death-watch by a well-known industry pundit. His argument was a simple one: Barnes & Noble had just launched their website, and we had only 125 employees at the time, and something like $60 million in annual sales.

So his point was that you'd awakened a sleeping giant and filled it with a fierce resolve?

Exactly. They had 30,000 employees at that time, and $3 billion in sales. His message was, Amazon has had a good two-year run, but it's over. They're toast. The title of his report was actually "Amazon.Toast." It got picked up by the media, and it was pretty much everywhere, because we were sort of a poster child Internet company. To a person, I think, every one of our people got called by a parent—usually their mother—asking, "Are you okay? What's this about Amazon dot Toast?"

We had an all-hands meeting—which was very easy to do with only 125 people—and said, "Forget about this. We can't be thinking about how Barnes & Noble has so much more in the way of resources than we do." I told everyone, "Yes, you should wake up every morning terrified with your sheets drenched in sweat, but not because you're afraid of our competitors. Be afraid of our customers, because those are the folks who have the money. Our competitors are never going to send us money."

Since then we've made a number of decisions siding with the customer that have been questioned by well-meaning critics, journalists, Wall Street analysts, and industry analysts. I'm talking about things like free shipping, relentlessly lowering prices, Amazon Prime. And every time we make one of those and get broadly criticized for it and then it works, we get a little more credibility.

What would you say has been the nature of your biggest strategic mistakes?

I think most big errors are errors of omission rather than errors of commission. They are the ones that companies never get held to account for—the times when they were in a position to notice something and act on it, had the skills and competencies or could have acquired them, and yet failed to do so. It's the opposite of sticking to your knitting: It's when you shouldn't have stuck to your knitting but you did.

It's hard to imagine how you could spot those errors of omission in time to hold a management team accountable. What are you doing to prevent them?

One useful habit is to ask the question, "Why not?" When something seems like an opportunity—it seems like you have the skills, and maybe some kind of advantage, and you think it's a big area—you will always get asked the question, "Why? Why do that?" But "Why not?" is an equally valid question. And there may be good reasons why not—maybe you don't have the capital resources, or parts of your current business require so much focus at this key juncture that it would be irresponsible. In that case, if somebody asked, "Why not?" you would say, "Here's why not . . ." But that question doesn't get asked. It's an asymmetry that is linked to those errors of omission.

If you are determined to avoid errors of omission, doesn't that put you at great risk of taking on too much and spreading resources too thin?

What you really want to do companywide is maximize the number of experiments you can do per given unit of time. If something's really big—like the big bet we've made on Amazon Web Services—then sure, you can do only a limited number of those, so you spend more time thinking about them and talking them through. Somebody wears the black hat and makes the case for why not to do it, and somebody else puts on the white hat and says why it is actually a good thing to do. But since the outcomes of all these things are uncertain, if you can figure out how to conduct an experiment, you can make more bets. So the key, really, is reducing the cost of the experiments. We have a group called Web Lab that is constantly experimenting with the user interface on the website, getting statistical data from real usage patterns about which interfaces work best. That is a huge laboratory for us, and we've put a lot of energy into trying to figure out how to be very low cost with those experiments so that we can run a much larger number of them.

As a practical matter, sometimes it's very, very hard to dramatically reduce the cost of experimentation. There are areas where conducting an experiment is still, in terms of cost, tantamount to just doing it. But you should always be trying to do that. You should be making guesses and then finding out at lowest cost whether or not they are needle movers.

How often do experiments turn out wildly different from what you expected?

Sometimes you make guesses and you think, When we launch this, people are going to love it. And they don't. We launched a feature—I forget what we named it— where we'd take your purchase history and then find, out of our millions of other customers, the one customer whose purchase history was the closest match. You could push a button, and we'd show you all the things that your doppelgänger had bought that you had not. No one used it. Our history is full of things like that, where we came up with an innovation that we thought was really cool, and the customers didn't care. Fortunately, there are also quite a few that went the other way. Back when we first launched the Associates program, we thought it was a nice thing to do but had relatively low expectations for it. This is our marketing program that lets other sites earn affiliate fees by sending buyers to us. It was the first program of its kind, and it dramatically exceeded our expectations. Very quickly we doubled down on it as a favored marketing program. And it's continuing to be very successful 11 years later.

At the same time, you have to recognize that there are times when you can't put a toe in the water; you have to leap in with both feet. You have to say, "This is going to be expensive—and that means we're going to have to make it work." You allow that you might take lots of twists and turns on the details, but you really commit yourself to the objective. And by the way, it's very fun to have the kind of culture where people are willing to take these leaps—it's the opposite of the "institutional no." It's the institutional yes. People say, "We're going to do this. We're going to figure out a way."

How does that square with the emphasis you place on taking your cues from the early results of experiments?

My observation on that would be that it's important to be stubborn on the vision and flexible on the details. I talked about the evolution of our marketplace business—that's a good example of where we were relentless on the vision. We made a lot of twists and turns in the execution. We worked on it for a few years. But we didn't give up on the vision. I think if you believe that a particular customer set is important, like sellers in that case, and you believe you have identified what some of their nontransient needs will be, and you believe the addressable market is big enough for it to matter—if you really believe those things, then it pays to be stubborn in pursuing that.

As the business grew and moved into new areas, you must have felt challenged to keep up on a personal level. What have you had to learn along the way?

Something we haven't talked about, but that is super important in our culture, is the focus on defect reduction and execution. It's one of the reasons that we have been successful for customers. That is something I had to learn about.

That's not your natural strength?

Well, by "learn" I mean I literally learned a bunch of techniques, like Six Sigma and lean manufacturing and other incredibly useful approaches. I'm very detail oriented by nature, so I have the right instincts to be an acceptable operator, but I didn't have the tools to create repeatable processes and to know where those processes made sense. Before I started Amazon, I was with a quantitative hedge fund. That work is very disciplined and very analytical, but it's not a question of designing a repeatable process. It's not like a car-manufacturing plant, where the work has to be done in a defect-free way, in the same way over and over and over—or anyway, that piece of it is not as important. But here, that execution focus is a big factor, and you can see it in our financial metrics over the past ten years. It's very obvious when, for instance, we look at the number of customer contacts per unit sold. Our customers don't contact us unless something's wrong, so we want that number to move down—and it has gone down every year for 12 years. That's big-time process management. We try to implement those kinds of processes in various places. They're most naturally applied in our fulfillment centers and in customer service and so on, but we've actually found that they can be useful in a bunch of different things.

When you are inexperienced with disciplined process management, you initially think that it's equivalent to bureaucracy. But effective process is not bureaucracy. Bureaucracy is senseless processing—and we've had some of that, too.

What else has been critical to your ability to grow as a manager and leader? Often, entrepreneurs aren't able to scale with the businesses they found.

I don't know that I have anything profound to say about that. When you start out, it's a one-person thing, at least on the first day, and you're not only figuring out what to do but actually doing it. At a certain point the company gets bigger, and you get to where you're mostly figuring out what to do but not how it's done. Eventually you get to the point where you're mostly figuring out who is going to do it, not even what to do. So one way to think about this is as a transition of questions, from "How?" to "What?" to "Who?" It's not necessarily a conscious thing; circumstances dictate it. As things get bigger, I don't think you can operate any other way. So the question for any senior executive is, basically, "Are you progressing along that curve at the right rate?"

Now, of course, I'm oversimplifying, because the reality is that you continue to dive deep in selected areas. I've never met what I think of as a good executive who does not choose certain highly leveraged activities—some area they consider so important that they will inspect it all the way down to the how stage.

What's your deep-dive area?

When it comes to the way we relentlessly drive down our consumer-facing pricing, I still continually launder and inspect that and talk to the people who do the work all the way through that whole chain. I need to be sure that we are in fact competitive and focused on offering our customers the lowest possible prices. That's one of the things I think is so highly leveraged that I am involved from heading level one all the way to heading level five.

Is there anyone in the company who can say no to you?

I'm actually thinking, Who doesn't? We have many strong executives, so not even just my direct reports but beneath them. We have an informal atmosphere, which I think helps people tell me no—and not just me. It's also really important that they be able to say what they think to their senior vice president or vice president and so on. An informal atmosphere, I think, is a huge benefit.

That doesn't mean we don't have raucous debates and get angry with each other occasionally. Intensity is important. I always tell people that our culture is friendly and intense, but if push comes to shove, we'll settle for intense. But there is no contradiction between being intense and having fun. You can absolutely do that. That's what we try to achieve, and at our best it is what we achieve. We'll have some big problems, we'll get together, and we'll laugh about them. Sometimes it's dark humor, but it's either laugh or cry. And then we try to work our way through them. I think there's a lot of value in having fun, even though in a more formal culture some of our meetings might look undisciplined. In a one-hour meeting we may spend ten minutes of it joking around, and I'm often the worst offender. I'll laugh and say, "This reminds me of . . ." and get us off on some story. Eventually somebody says, "Well, that is very interesting, but you do see we have an agenda . . ." And I think that works out great.

Originally published in October 2007
Reprint R0710C

How Industries Change

ANITA M. MCGAHAN

Executive Summary

IT'S FAIRLY OBVIOUS: To make intelligent investments
within your organization, you need to understand how
your whole industry is changing. But such knowledge is
not always easy to come by. Companies misread clues
and arrive at false conclusions all the time.

To truly understand where your industry is headed,
you have to take a long-term, high-level look at the context in which you do business, says Boston University professor Anita McGahan. She studied a variety of businesses from a cross section of industries over a ten-year
period, examining how industry structure affects business
profitability and investor returns. Her research suggests
that industries evolve along one of four distinct trajectories—*radical, progressive, creative,* and *intermediating*—
that set boundaries on what will generate profits in a
business. These four trajectories are defined by two types

51

of threats. The first is when new, outside alternatives threaten to weaken or make obsolete *core activities* that have historically generated profits for an industry. The second is when an industry's *core assets*—its resources, knowledge, and brand capital—fail to generate value as they once did.

Industries undergo radical change when core assets and core activities are both threatened with obsolescence; they experience progressive change when neither are jeopardized. Creative change occurs when core assets are under threat but core activities are stable, and intermediating change happens when core activities are threatened while core assets retain their capacity to create value.

If your company's innovation strategy is not aligned with your industry's change trajectory, your plan for achieving returns on invested capital cannot succeed, McGahan says. But if you understand which path you're on, you can determine which strategies will succeed and which will backfire.

You can't make intelligent investments within your organization unless you understand how your whole industry is changing. If the industry is in the midst of radical change, you'll eventually have to dismantle old businesses. If the industry is experiencing incremental change, you'll probably need to reinvest in your core. The need to understand change in your industry may seem obvious, but such knowledge is not always easy to come by. Companies misread clues and arrive at false conclusions all the time. Sotheby's, for example, invested in online auctions (its own Web site as well as a venture with Amazon) as if the Internet were just another channel; in truth, the new technology represented a fundamental shock to the industry's structure.

To truly understand where your industry is headed, you have to shut out the noise from the popular business press and the pressure of immediate competitive threats to take a longer-term look at the context in which you do business. That is what some of my colleagues and I did. The research described in this article is based on a high-level look at a variety of businesses from a broad cross section of U.S. industries. The research, which began in the early 1990s and continues today, originally focused on how industry structure affects business profitability and investor returns. This statistical analysis yielded several hypotheses about how industries evolve, which were then tested and refined in a series of case studies on industry structure, industry change, and competitive advantage.

The conclusion, which I'll oversimplify here for the sake of clarity, is that industries evolve along four distinct trajectories—radical, progressive, creative, and intermediating.[1] Moreover, a firm's strategy—its plan for achieving a return on invested capital—cannot succeed unless it is aligned with the industry's change trajectory. The four trajectories set boundaries on what will generate profits in a business. Many companies have incurred losses because they tried to innovate outside of those boundaries. One of the most famous examples is Xerox, which is legendary for its innovations and for its struggle to harvest profits from them. By the mid 1980s, the copier manufacturing industry had matured around a business model that emphasized creative "hit products." Meanwhile, the personal computing industry was in its infancy, and even though Xerox PARC had pioneered PC inventions such as the graphical user interface and the mouse, the company was unable to make inroads in this burgeoning industry that required an entirely new set of business activities.

No innovation strategy works for every company in every industry. But if you understand the nature of change in your industry, you can determine which strategies are likely to succeed and which will backfire.

Four Trajectories of Change

Before we look at the four trajectories of industry evolution in depth, it is worthwhile to recognize that they are defined by two types of threats of obsolescence. The first is a threat to the industry's core activities—the activities that have historically generated profits for the industry. These are threatened when they become less relevant to suppliers and customers because of some new, outside alternative. In the auto industry, for example, many dealerships are finding that their traditional sales activities are less valued by consumers, who are going online for data on the characteristics, performance, and prices of the cars they want. The second is a threat to the industry's core assets—the resources, knowledge, and brand capital that have historically made the organization unique. These are threatened if they fail to generate value as they once did. In the pharmaceutical industry, for instance, blockbuster drugs are constantly under threat as patents expire and new drugs are developed.

The exhibit "Trajectories of Industry Change" maps the relationships between these two threats and the following four change trajectories. *Radical* change occurs when an industry's core assets and core activities are both threatened with obsolescence. This trajectory is closest to the concept of disruptive change that Harvard's Clayton M. Christensen discusses. Under this scenario, the knowledge and brand capital built up in the industry erode, and so do customer and supplier relationships. During the 1980s and 1990s, an estimated 19% of U.S. industries went through some stage of radical change. A good example is the travel business. Agencies' core activities and core assets came under fire as the airlines implemented systems to enhance direct price competition (such as SABRE and other reservations systems) and as the agencies' clients turned to Web-enabled systems (such as Expedia, Orbitz, and Travelocity) that offered new value (online monitoring of available flights and fares, for instance).

Trajectories of Industry Change

When determining which type of change your industry is going through—and, no doubt, it is going through some type of transformation—you need to consider whether there are threats to your industry's **core activities** *(the recurring actions your company performs that attract and retain suppliers and buyers) and to your industry's* **core assets** *(the durable resources, including intangibles, that make your company more efficient at performing core activities).*

		Core Activities	
		Threatened	Not threatened
Core Assets	Threatened	**Radical Change** *Everything is up in the air.* Examples: makers of landline telephone handsets, overnight letter-delivery carriers, and travel agencies	**Creative Change** *The industry is constantly redeveloping assets and resources.* Examples: the motion picture industry, sports team ownership, and investment banking
	Not threatened	**Intermediating Change** *Relationships are fragile.* Examples: automobile dealerships, investment brokerages, and auction houses	**Progressive Change** *Companies implement incremental testing and adapt to feedback.* Examples: online auctions, commercial airlines, and long-haul trucking

When neither core assets nor core activities are threatened, the industry's change trajectory is *progressive*. Over the past 20 years, this has been by far the most common trajectory; about 43% of U.S. industries were changing progressively, including long-haul trucking and commercial airlines. In those industries, the basic assets, activities, and underlying technologies remained stable. Innovators like Yellow Roadway, Southwest, and JetBlue succeeded not because the incumbents' strengths became obsolete but because the upstart firms had smart insights about how to optimize efficiency.

The other two change trajectories—*creative* and *intermediating*—have been neglected in the management literature, possibly because of their nuances. Creative change occurs when core assets are under threat but core activities are stable. This means that companies must continually find ways to restore their assets while protecting ongoing customer and supplier relationships; think of movie studios churning out new films or oil companies mining for new wells. About 6% of all U.S. industries are on a creative change trajectory.

Intermediating change occurs when core activities are threatened with obsolescence—customer and supplier relationships are stretched and fragile—while core assets retain their capacity to create value. Sotheby's, for instance, is as good as it ever was at assessing fine works of art, but, because of the technology that made eBay possible, the auction house's matchmaking activity no longer creates as much value. The challenge under intermediating change is to find ways to preserve knowledge, brand capital, and other valuable assets while fundamentally changing relationships with customers and with suppliers. During the 1980s and 1990s, approximately

32% of U.S. industries went through some form of intermediating change. (See the exhibit "A Fair Share?".)

Radical Change

Radical transformation occurs when both core activities and core assets are threatened with obsolescence. The

---

A Fair Share?

The four change trajectories are not at all evenly distributed among industries. Surprisingly, given the time and attention much of the management literature devotes to it, radical change affects less than one-fifth of all industries. More prevalent are progressive and intermediating change. The percentages shown are estimates of the distribution of change trajectories among U.S. industries between 1980 and 1999, based on variability in revenues and assets among large firms.

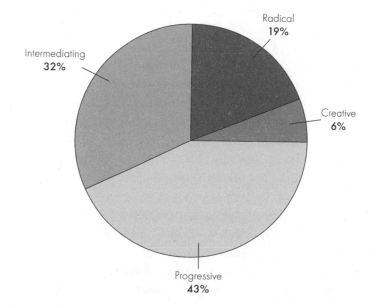

Radical
19%

Intermediating
32%

Creative
6%

Progressive
43%

relevance of an industry's established capabilities and resources is diminished by some outside alternative; relationships with buyers and suppliers come under attack; and companies are eventually thrown into crisis. Radical industry evolution is relatively unusual. It normally occurs following the mass introduction of some new technology. It can also happen when there are regulatory changes (as in the long-haul, trunk-route airline industry of the 1970s, for example) or simply because of changes in taste (U.S. consumers' retreat from cigarettes over the past 20 years, for instance).

An industry on a radical change trajectory is entirely transformed—but not overnight. It usually takes decades for change to become clear and play out. The end result is a completely reconfigured—usually diminished—industry. The overnight letter-delivery business is currently in the early phases of a radical transformation that began about ten years ago. As Internet usage has become more prevalent, e-mail (especially securely encrypted e-mail) has loomed as a threat to this industry. Yet the volume of overnight letters is increasing; business is still thriving, because the threat is still in its infancy.

That is part of the good news associated with radical transformation: Industries that are on a radical change trajectory often remain profitable for a long time, especially if the companies in these industries scale back their commitments accordingly. Businesses also have time to develop strategic options that can be exercised in the future if they recognize the trajectory they are on early enough. For example, Federal Express's acquisition of Kinko's will help FedEx create deeper relationships with small and midsize businesses that need document storage, management, and dissemination services.

The only reasonable approach to radical change is to focus on the endgame and its implications for your company's current strategy. Exiting isn't the sole option; sometimes a few survivors can sustain profitable positions after others leave the industry. The computer mainframe business, for example, is still quite large despite the threat from PC and workstation manufacturers.

To consider the best strategy when your industry is on a radical change trajectory, look at your productivity figures, the pace and timing of the transition in the industry, and buyers' switching costs. Early-moving companies might employ a staggered strategy—pursuing incremental improvements to established businesses' activities and conducting selective experiments in developing new assets. That is how encyclopedia companies responded to the radical threat that online search engines posed: They experimented with new electronic products and services while creating new distribution channels, marketing their existing products aggressively, and updating their inventory management systems.

Historically, many organizations confronted with radical change in their industries have abandoned their established positions and moved into emerging lines of business—incurring enormous risk in the process. Several typewriter makers, for instance, attempted to enter the PC manufacturing business only to cut short their efforts as the demands of the emerging industry became clearer. (IBM succeeded with this strategy, but its success in the PC industry was closely related to its experience in other areas of computing.) The alternative—reinvesting in the established industry—is also risky because it commits the firm to an approach that may become unprofitable. Companies dealing with radical transformation must accept the inevitability of the change and chart a course that maximizes returns without accelerating commitment to the troubled business— much easier said than done.

Intermediating Change

Intermediating change is more common than radical industry evolution. It typically occurs when buyers and suppliers have new options because they have gained unprecedented access to information. The core activities of industries on an intermediating change trajectory are threatened. But the core assets of these industries— knowledge, brand capital, patents, or even specialized factory equipment—retain most of their value if they are used in new ways. In effect, industries are on an intermediating change trajectory when their business activities for dealing in both downstream and upstream markets are simultaneously threatened. Intermediating change is occurring in auto dealerships, for example, for a number of reasons. First, traditional auto sales activities are becoming less relevant because of the Internet and because vehicles now last so long that consumers buy cars less frequently. Second, car manufacturers are seeking closer relationships with drivers and, as a result, are starting to share the management of customer relations with their dealers; in some cases, they're trying to take over customer relations completely. Finally, individual dealers are losing control of inventory management as IT and sophisticated financing create economies of scope that can be exploited only by larger, integrated companies.

Managing a company in an industry that is experiencing intermediating change is extraordinarily difficult. Of all the change trajectories described in this article, this one is perhaps the most challenging because companies must simultaneously preserve their valuable assets and restructure their key relationships.

Executives tend to underestimate the threat to their core activities by assuming that longtime customers are still satisfied and that old supplier relationships are still relevant. In reality, these relationships have probably become fragile. The value of core assets often escalates, which compounds managers' confusion. For example, auction houses initially had a flurry of heightened interest in their accumulated appraisal experience because eBay had created so much excitement about auctioning.

During periods of intermediating change, pressure in the industry tends to build until it hits a breaking point, and then relationships break down dramatically only to be temporarily reconstituted until the cycle is repeated. Consider large brokerage firms. They had long confronted criticism about conflicts of interest in their analyst organizations. But the straws that broke the camel's back were the recent market downturn and accounting scandals—both of which were tied to fundamental changes in the information available to investors and companies seeking investment capital. The core assets in investment brokerage—including the systems for evaluating securities and for processing trades—retained their value, yet old relationships no longer offered the same opportunities to generate profits.

Companies facing intermediating change must find unconventional ways to extract value from their core resources. They may diversify by entering a new business or even a new industry. Or they may sell off assets or services to former competitors. In the music industry, for instance, recording companies are beginning to sell their services à la carte to aspiring musicians rather than make huge investments in the artists up front and incur all the costs of artist development (radio promotions, choreography, and image management, among other expenses). The customer and the activities have changed, but the core resource—the recording companies' ability to develop new artists—retains its value. In another example, some traditional auctioneers, threatened by eBay, have capitalized on their appraisal expertise online; for a fee, they will certify the value of the wares being exchanged on the Internet. By reconfiguring old assets in new ways, these companies are dealing effectively with intermediation.

Initial returns under this change trajectory may be relatively high and then drop dramatically only to recover temporarily. The recording companies' profits, for example, have been volatile as the companies adapt to intermediation with varying levels of success. A plateau in performance can create the illusion that reinvestment in the business as usual is a good idea. But organizations that recognize the trajectory their industry is on can turn relatively calm periods into opportunities for strategic transformation.

Creative Change

In industries on a creative change trajectory, relationships with customers and suppliers are generally stable, but assets turn over constantly. The film production industry is a good example. Larger production companies enjoy ongoing relationships with actors, agents, theater owners, and cable television executives. Within this network, they produce and distribute new films all the time. This combination of unstable assets (new films) and stable relationships (with buyers and suppliers) makes it possible to deliver superior performance over the long term. Indeed, the top companies in creative change industries usually retain their standing for long periods.

Other industries evolving on creative trajectories include pharmaceuticals, oil and gas exploration, and prepackaged software. In pharmaceuticals, companies research, develop, and test new drugs and then use their administrative and marketing skills to commercialize them. In oil and gas exploration, companies manage their portfolios of exploration ventures and maintain relationships with refineries and distributors. In the prepackaged software industry, developers create and test multiple applications in the hopes that one or more will become a killer app. By applying well-honed user-testing and marketing skills, the industry leaders perpetuate their success.

The creative change trajectory, like the intermediating trajectory, has not been studied extensively. It is easy to mistake it for radical change, despite the stability of relationships within the network. When this mistake is made, companies can overreact and neglect important relationships that are critical to their profitability. For example, some pharmaceutical companies became so focused on emerging methods of drug discovery that they invested capital exclusively in new research relationships and did not develop appropriate sales forces in new markets.

Innovation under creative change occurs in fits and starts. Although there are several long-standing formulas for making hit movies, for example, occasionally a new genre or technical approach to filmmaking emerges. Similarly, companies in the pharmaceutical industry have been experimenting with new methods of drug discovery over the last 15 years. Despite these changes, the companies that lead these industries are not new entrants. They have retained their strength by capitalizing on their networks of relationships.

There are many ways for companies in an industry on a creative change trajectory to generate strong returns on invested capital. For instance, the leading companies in these industries tend to spread the risk of new-project development over a portfolio of initiatives. As a result, their returns are less volatile than those of smaller competitors. Other tactics include outsourcing project management and development tasks.

Progressive Change

Progressive evolution is like creative evolution in that buyers, suppliers, and the industry's incumbents have incentives to preserve the status quo. The difference is that core assets are not threatened with obsolescence under progressive change, so industries on this trajectory are more stable than those on a creative change trajectory. Today's discount retailing, long-haul trucking, and commercial airline industries are evolving in this way.

Progressive evolution is most similar to the kind of change that Christensen refers to as "sustaining." Progress occurs, and technology can have an enormous impact, but it happens within the existing framework of the business. Core resources tend to appreciate rather than depreciate over time. Progressive change doesn't mean that change is minor or even that it is slow. Over time, incremental changes can lead to major improvements and major changes. Think of what has happened in discount retailing over the last ten years. Wal-Mart's cumulative impact has been extraordinary, and the company has developed unprecedented clout. But the retailer developed that advantage by deepening existing customer and supplier relationships, not by seeking out entirely new ones.

The most profitable corporate strategies in progressive change industries generally involve carving out distinct positions based on geographic, technical, or marketing expertise. The goal is to build resources and capabilities steadily and incrementally. Companies rarely get into brinkmanship or eyeball-to-eyeball competition, and they don't have to put large amounts of capital at risk before learning whether an innovation creates value. Instead, their performance depends on their quick responses to feedback. Southwest Airlines, for instance, tests new flight routes but isn't afraid to pull out if a route ultimately doesn't work under the company's approach to air travel.

Successful companies in progressive change industries tend to be viewed by the financial community as minimally risky with the potential for only moderate returns. Over the long run, though, these companies can actually create very large total returns for investors. *Money* has reported that the two companies that had generated the greatest total return to shareholders during the magazine's 25-year history were none other than Wal-Mart and Southwest.

Which Trajectory Are You On?

Identifying your industry's evolutionary trajectory on the fly is difficult. It is easy to become distracted or confused by conventional wisdom, customer demands, and competitors' moves. To ensure accuracy, your analysis must be focused and systematic.

The first step is to define your industry. You can begin by identifying the companies in your industry that share common buyers and suppliers. Many economists use a

5% rule to assess whether the commonality is sufficient to qualify the firms as direct competitors: If a 5% price fluctuation by one company causes customers or suppliers to switch to another company, the businesses qualify as direct competitors. When a group of companies intend to appeal to the same buyers and rely on the same suppliers, you have additional evidence that they are direct competitors. And when companies use similar technologies to create value, it is likely that they qualify as direct competitors.

The second step is to define the industry's core assets and activities. Here is an easy way to test whether something is core: If it were eradicated today, would profits be lower a year from now, despite efforts to work around what's missing? If the answer is yes, then it definitely qualifies. In the auctioneering industry, for example, the capacity to evaluate works of art is a core activity. In the soft-drink industry, Coca-Cola's brand is a core asset. The disappearance of either of these capabilities would seriously damage profitability in their respective industries.

The third step is to determine whether the core assets and activities are threatened with obsolescence. To qualify, the threat must make core assets and activities potentially irrelevant to profitability. It must be significant enough to jeopardize the survival of at least one industry leader and widespread enough to influence every company in the industry. Once you know whether core activities and assets are threatened, you can identify which of the four trajectories applies to the industry you are studying.

The final step in the diagnosis is to evaluate the phase of the evolutionary trajectory. This step is important: Industry change generally takes place over a long period, and the options for dealing with change typically drop off sharply through each phase. (See "The Industry Life Cycle Revisited" at the end of this article.)

It is also essential to note that an industry generally evolves along just one trajectory at a time. It almost always starts out on either a progressive or creative trajectory because, collectively, companies in the industry can't capture value without a clear model for organizing their core activities. Over time, the industry may feel pressure to change these activities—driven by, for example, customer demands and new technologies. The threat of obsolescence can catapult the industry on to either a radical or an intermediating trajectory. As the industry restructures its core activities and assets, the threat of obsolescence may fade, marking the industry's transition back to a progressive or creative trajectory. A company that has survived these transitions can sometimes retain profitability, although it almost always must operate at a smaller scale and with a very different approach.

Industries do not shift their trajectories very often; no industry that I have studied has shifted between evolutionary paths more than once in ten years. So it is a good bet that a given industry has been on a single evolutionary trajectory for at least a few years. And while it is sometimes possible for individual companies to influence the trajectory of an entire industry, the effort required is almost always too great to be worthwhile, and failure can be devastating to the company's profitability or even its survival.

Capitalizing on Industry Evolution

Understanding industry change can do more than help you avoid mistakes. The rules under each trajectory can help you forecast early on how change will occur in your industry—and help you determine how to exploit change as it occurs. It would be impossible to list here all the possible contingencies for change on each trajectory and at each stage. But here are a few general insights:

ANALYZING RADICAL AND INTERMEDIATING CHANGE

As noted earlier, companies operating in an industry that is on a radical or intermediating change trajectory must perform a balancing act—aggressively pursuing profits in the near term while avoiding investments that could later prevent them from ramping down their commitments. To get the right balance, put yourself in the suppliers' shoes as well as in those of the buyers. What new options are emerging?

Take the example of auto dealerships, which are on an intermediating change trajectory. They are locked into multiyear pacts with the manufacturers, their suppliers. Yet the intermediation of the dealers presents new opportunities for the automakers to relate to consumers: What are the trade-offs for the manufacturers if they advertise collaboratively with the dealerships rather than directly to consumers? How can the carmakers pull off something like this without violating their contracts with the dealers? Only with unconventional thinking— beyond standard market research and advertising plans—can the manufacturers find answers to these questions.

Radical and intermediating change also call for new ways of dealing with competitive threats. Instead of viewing rivals in conventional terms, consider whether you can use alliances to protect common interests and defend against new competition from outsiders—or to facilitate consolidation. When some regions of the U.S. became overcrowded with auto dealerships, affiliated car lots (Honda dealers in adjacent towns, for instance) merged.

Under radical and intermediating change, it is also important to interpret conflict within your organization in a new way. "Civil wars" can emerge within an organization as divisions with exposure to different segments of the business develop opposing views about the nature and pace of change. It is uncanny how frequently this happens. Strong, central leadership is required to deal with the problem effectively.

SURVIVING RADICAL AND CREATIVE CHANGE

Under these conditions, it is smart to evaluate how quickly your core assets are depreciating. The easiest way to do this is to identify how much you are spending to renew them. Investing in a full-blown cost-accounting effort is worthwhile since the value of your assets may vary across different segments of the business in surprising ways. The goal of this analysis should be to distinguish the segments in which you can protect your competitive position from those in which your position will erode quickly. Often, this assessment yields important information about the value of intellectual property and how it can be guarded more intensively. For example, a film studio might discover that, in some geographies, losses from video piracy outweigh the potential profits from distributing content, at retail, on videotape or DVD.

To navigate radical and creative change trajectories successfully, companies must have the mettle to disappoint some buyers and suppliers, regardless of their track records, if the risks are too high. Despite Marlon

Brando's box-office successes during the 1950s, film studios were reluctant to work with him because of his personal idiosyncrasies. The stakes in developing new films
are simply too great for producers to take many risks.
Because of the volatility of new-asset development, it is
also crucial to cultivate relationships with investors to
ensure quick access to capital when a worthwhile project
comes around.

MANAGING PROGRESSIVE CHANGE

Progressive change is not simple to manage, despite the
fact that neither core assets nor core activities are
threatened. The accumulated impact of incremental
changes can raise the standards for doing business to the
point where only a handful of companies are competitive. For example, the standard-bearers in discount
retailing (Wal-Mart and Target among them) have
relentlessly managed incremental changes in activities
for decades. As a result, only a few national retailers have
competitive cost structures on a large scale. Ultimately,
one of the most successful strategies for companies in
industries on a progressive change trajectory is to
develop a system of interrelated activities that are defen-
sible because of their compounding effects on profits,
not because they are hard to understand or replicate.
Consider that very little about Wal-Mart's approach is
secret. The company's efficiencies have accumulated
ever since Sam Walton built his first distribution centers
decades ago.

ADAPTING TO THE STAGES OF CHANGE

As we've noted, all four trajectories typically unfold over
decades, which means organizations have time to outline

strategic options for the future. As change happens, fighting it is almost always too costly to be worthwhile. In the late stages, companies invite trouble by sticking with outdated budget systems and cost-accounting processes. Organizations must reconfigure themselves for lower revenue growth and develop the ability to move activities and resources out of the business.

DIVERSIFYING YOUR BUSINESS

Some of the most exciting opportunities associated with industry evolution relate to diversification across industries. By participating in more than one industry on a progressive trajectory, Wal-Mart has enhanced the effects of its powerful distribution systems. And with its acquisition of Kinko's, FedEx has diversified in response to radical change. Some of the major challenges of diversification have to do with sharing core activities and core assets across divisions on different trajectories, and developing clear lines of authority for resolving disputes between divisions as their industries create different investment requirements. It is virtually impossible to diversify profitably without understanding the differences in the trajectories and phases of industry change.

THE TRAJECTORIES OUTLINED above can help you anticipate how change will unfold in your industry—and how to take advantage of opportunities as they emerge. To get out from under industry threats, your company must cultivate a deep understanding of how changes to the industry will unfold over time. How will buyer and seller relationships be affected? And are intangible assets like brand capital and knowledge capital truly adaptable across industries? The work of systematically analyzing the business environment is not easy, but the payoff is great: better strategic decision making for your company.

Notes

1. This article builds on the author's "How Industries Evolve," *Business Strategy Review,* Autumn 2000.

The Industry Life Cycle Revisited

ONCE YOU'VE DETERMINED which change trajectory your industry is on, you'll need to figure out which phase of change the industry is experiencing. The classic industry life cycle model is relevant for understanding the phases of progressive and creative change. But this model does not apply to industries that are experiencing radical or intermediating change.

In the traditional life cycle model, industries begin in a period of *fragmentation* as companies experiment with different approaches to a market. The companies offer a variety of products and operate at low volumes. They tend to be entrepreneurial, private, and focused on serving narrow geographic areas. Over time, the industry experiences a *shakeout,* usually because a specific business model achieves greater legitimacy than any other. Competitors become more efficient, the volume of sales increases, and the industry generates unprecedented value for suppliers and buyers. When industries reach *maturity,* sales growth slows, and leaders often lock their positions. As the volume of sales drops, industries move into *decline*. In this phase, companies often search for incremental improvements in efficiency to recover profitability. (See "The Traditional Model.")

But if you apply this model in industries that are experiencing radical or intermediating change, you may end up trying to renew your position in an industry that will no longer generate significant returns. Or you may end up missing opportunities in both the established and emerging industries.

The Traditional Model

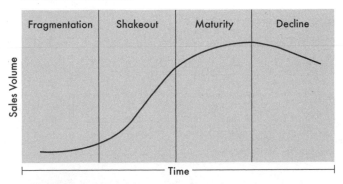

An Alternate Model

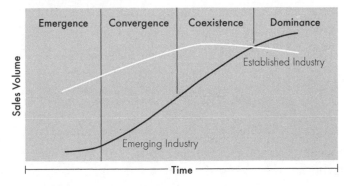

A more accurate model for those on radical or intermediating trajectories is the one below, which reflects
changes in the ways buyers and suppliers respond to the
level of the threat of obsolescence. (See "An Alternate
Model.") During an initial period of *emergence,* upstart
firms warrant attention but may not be significant enough
to prompt established companies to restructure. As the
new approach *converges* in volume, established companies may react by reconfiguring some of their activities.
During a period of *coexistence,* buyers and suppliers
become increasingly sophisticated at evaluating the new
approach, and as a result, new opportunities for value
creation may emerge even in the old industry. During a
final phase of *dominance,* the industry's products and
services are evaluated on new criteria that reflect the
popularity of the new approach.

Originally published in October 2004
Reprint R0410E

Finding Your Next Core Business

CHRIS ZOOK

Executive Summary

HOW DO YOU KNOW when your core needs to
change? And how do you determine what should
replace it? From an in-depth study of 25 companies, the
author, a strategy consultant, has discovered that it's possible to measure the vitality of a business's core. If it
needs reinvention, he says, the best course is to mine hidden assets.

Some of the 25 companies were in deep crisis when
they began the process of redefining themselves. But,
says Zook, management teams can learn to recognize
early signs of erosion. He offers five diagnostic questions
with which to evaluate the customers, key sources of differentiation, profit pools, capabilities, and organizational
culture of your core business.

The next step is strategic regeneration. In four-fifths of
the companies Zook examined, a hidden asset was the

centerpiece of the new strategy. He provides a map for identifying the hidden assets in your midst, which tend to fall into three categories: undervalued business platforms, untapped insights into customers, and underexploited capabilities. The Swedish company Dometic, for example, was manufacturing small absorption refrigerators for boats and RVs when it discovered a hidden asset: its understanding of, and access to, customers in the RV market. The company took advantage of a boom in that market to refocus on complete systems for live-in vehicles. The Danish company Novozymes, which produced relatively low-tech commodity enzymes such as those used in detergents, realized that its underutilized biochemical capability in genetic and protein engineering was a hidden asset and successfully refocused on creating bioengineered specialty enzymes.

Your next core business is not likely to announce itself with fanfare. Use the author's tools to conduct an internal audit of possibilities and pinpoint your new focus.

IT IS A WONDER how many management teams fail to exploit, or even perceive, the full potential of the basic businesses they are in. Company after company prematurely abandons its core in the pursuit of some hot market or sexy new idea, only to see the error of its ways—often when it's too late to reverse course. Bausch & Lomb is a classic example. Its eagerness to move beyond contact lenses took it into dental products, skin care, and even hearing aids in the 1990s. Today B&L has divested itself of all those businesses at a loss, and is scrambling in the category it once dominated (where Johnson & Johnson now leads). And yet it's also true that no core endures forever. Sticking with an eroding core for too long, as Polaroid did, can be just as devastating. Both these companies were once darlings of Wall Street, each with an intelligent management team and a formerly dominant core. And in a sense, they made the same mistake: They misjudged the point their core business had reached in its life cycle and whether it was time to stay focused, expand, or move on.

How do you know when your core needs to change in some fundamental way? And how do you determine what the new core should be? These are the questions that have driven my conversations with senior managers and the efforts of my research team over the past three years. What we've discovered is that it is possible to measure the vitality remaining in a business's core—to see whether that core is truly exhausted or still has legs. We've also concluded from an in-depth study of companies that have redefined their cores (including Apple, IBM, De Beers, PerkinElmer, and 21 others) that there is a right way to go about reinvention. The surest route is not to venture far afield but to mine new value close to home; assets already in hand but peripheral to the core offer up the richest new cores.

This article discusses both these findings. It identifies the warning signs that a business is losing its potency and offers a way to diagnose the strength remaining in its core. It recounts the efforts of managers in a variety of settings who saw the writing on the wall and succeeded in transforming their companies. And, based on these and other cases, it maps the likely spots in a business where the makings of a new core might be found.

When It's Time for Deep Strategic Change

Not every company that falls on hard times needs to rethink its core strategy. On the contrary, declining performance in what was a thriving business can usually be chalked up to an execution shortfall. But when a strategy does turn out to be exhausted, it's generally for one of three reasons.

The first has to do with *profit pools*—the places along the total value chain of an industry where attractive profits are earned. If your company is targeting a shrinking or shifting profit pool, improving your ability to execute can accomplish only so much. Consider the position of Apple, whose share of the market for personal computers plummeted from 9% in 1995 to less than 3% in 2005. But more to the point, the entire profit pool in PCs steadily contracted during those years. If Apple had not moved its business toward digital music, its prospects might not look very bright. General Dynamics was in a similar situation in the 1990s, when defense spending declined sharply. To avoid being stranded by the receding profit pool, it sold off many of its units and redefined the company around just three core businesses where it held substantial advantages: submarines, electronics, and information systems.

The second reason is *inherently inferior economics.* These often come to light when a new competitor enters the field unburdened by structures and costs that an older company cannot readily shake off. General Motors saw this in competition with Toyota, just as Compaq did with Dell. Other well-known examples include Kmart (vis-à-vis Wal-Mart) and Xerox (vis-à-vis Canon). Occasionally a company sees the clouds gathering and is able to respond effectively. The Port of Singapore Authority (now PSA International), for example, fought off threats from Malaysia and other upstart competitors by slashing costs and identifying new ways to add value for customers. But sometimes the economics are driven by laws or entrenched arrangements that a company cannot change.

The third reason to rethink a core strategy is *a growth formula that cannot be sustained.* A manufacturer of a specialized consumer product—cell phones, say—might find its growth stalling as the market reaches saturation or competitors replicate its once unique source of differentiation. Or a retailer like Home Depot might see its growth slow as competitors like Lowe's catch up. A company that has prospered by simply reproducing its business model may run out of new territory to conquer: Think of the difficulties Wal-Mart has encountered as the cost-benefit ratio of further expansion shifts unfavorably. The core business of a mining company might expire as its mines become depleted. In all such circumstances, finding a new formula for growth depends on finding a new core.

For most of the companies my team and I studied, recognition that the core business had faltered came very late. The optical instruments maker PerkinElmer, the diamond merchant De Beers, the audio equipment manufacturer Harman International—these were all companies in deep crisis when they began their redefinition. Is it inevitable that companies will be blindsided in this way? Or can a management team learn to see early signs that its core strategy is losing relevance?

With that possibility in mind, it would seem reasonable to periodically assess the fundamental vitality of your business. The exhibit "Evaluate Your Core Business" offers a tool for doing so. Its first question looks at the core in terms of the customers it serves. How profitable are they—and how loyal? Arriving at the answers can be difficult, but no undertaking is more worthwhile; strategy goes nowhere unless it begins with the customer. The second question probes your company's key sources of differentiation and asks whether they are strengthening or eroding. The third focuses on your industry's

Evaluate Your Core Business

Five broad questions can help you determine when it is time to redefine your company's core business. For most companies, the answers to these questions can be found by examining the categories listed next to each one.

If the answers reveal that large shifts are about to take place in two or more of these five areas, your company is heading into turbulence; you need to reexamine the fundamentals of your core strategy and even the core itself.

Question	Take a close look at
1. What is the state of our core customers?	• profitability • market share • retention rate • measures of customer loyalty and advocacy • share of wallet
2. What is the state of our core differentiation?	• definition and metrics of differentiation • relative cost position • business models of emerging competitors • increasing or decreasing differentiation
3. What is the state of our industry's profit pools?	• size, growth, and stability • share of profit pools captured • boundaries • shifts and projections • high costs and prices
4. What is the state of our core capabilities?	• inventory of key capabilities • relative importance • gaps vis-à-vis competitors and vis-à-vis future core needs
5. What is the state of our culture and organization?	• loyalty and undesired attrition • capacity and stress points • alignment and agreement with objectives • energy and motivation • bottlenecks to growth

profit pools, a perspective that is often neglected in the quest for revenue and market share growth. Where are the best profits to be found? Who earns them now? How might that change? The fourth examines your company's capabilities—a topic we shall soon turn to—and the fifth assesses your organization's culture and readiness to change.

At the least, managers who go through this exercise tend to spot areas of weakness to be shored up. More dramatically, they may save a business from going under. Note, however, that no scoring system is attached to this diagnostic tool—there is no clearly defined point at which a prescription for strategic redefinition is issued. That would lend false precision to what must be a judgment call by a seasoned management team. The value of the exercise is to ensure that the right questions are taken into account and, by being asked consistently over time, highlight changes that may constitute growing threats to a company's core.

Recognizing the Makings of a New Core

Management teams react in different ways when they reach the conclusion that a core business is under severe threat. Some decide to defend the status quo. Others want to transform their companies all at once through a big merger. Some leap into a hot new market. Such strategies are inordinately risky. (Our analysis suggests that the odds of success are less than one in ten for the first two strategies, and only about one in seven for the third.) The companies we found to be most successful in remaking themselves proceeded in a way that left less to chance. Consider, for example, the transformation of the Swedish company Dometic.

Dometic's roots go back to 1922, when two engineering students named Carl Munters and Baltzar von Platen applied what was known as absorption technology to refrigeration. Whereas most household refrigerators use compressors driven by electric motors to generate cold, their refrigerator had no moving parts and no need for electricity; only a source of heat, as simple as a propane tank, was required. So the absorption refrigerator is particularly useful in places like boats and recreational vehicles, where electric current is hard to come by. In 1925 AB Electrolux acquired the patent rights. The division responsible for absorption refrigerators later became the independent Dometic Group.

By 1973 Dometic was still a small company, with revenues of just 80 million kronor (about U.S. $16.9 million). Worse, it was losing money. Then Sven Stork, an executive charged with fixing the ailing Electrolux product line, began to breathe new life into the business. Stork, who went on to become president and CEO of the company, moved aggressively into the hotel minibar market, where the absorption refrigerator's silent operation had a real advantage over conventional technology. Fueled by those sales, Dometic grew and was able to acquire some of its competitors.

The real breakthrough came when Stork's team focused more closely on the RV market, which was just then beginning to explode. The point wasn't to sell more refrigerators to the RV segment; the company's market share within that segment was already nearly 100%. Rather, it was to add other products to the Dometic line, such as air-conditioning, automated awnings, generators, and systems for cooking, lighting, sanitation, and water purification. As Stork explains, "We decided to make the RV into something that you could really live in.

The idea was obvious to people who knew the customers, yet it took a while to convince the manufacturers and especially the rest of our own organization." These moves fundamentally shifted the company's core. Dometic was no longer about absorption refrigeration: It was about RV interior systems and the formidable channel power gained by selling all its products through the same dealers and installers. That channel power allowed Dometic to pull off a move that enhanced its cost structure dramatically. The company streamlined its go-to-market approach in the United States by skipping a distribution layer that had always existed and approaching RV dealers directly. "We prepared for the risks like a military operation," Stork recalls, "and it was a fantastic hit. We were the only company large enough to pull this off. It let us kill off competitors faster than they could come out of the bushes." By 2005 Dometic had grown to KR 7.3 billion, or roughly U.S. $1.2 billion. No longer part of Electrolux (the private equity firm EQT bought it in 2001 and sold it to the investment firm BC Partners a few years later), the company was highly profitable and commanded 75% of the world market share for RV interior systems.

Dometic's story of growth and redefinition is especially instructive because it features all the elements we've seen repeatedly across the successful core-redefining companies we've studied. These are: (1) gradualism during transformation, (2) the discovery and use of hidden assets, (3) underlying leadership economics central to the strategy, and (4) a move from one repeatable formula that is unique to the company to another. "Gradualism" refers to the fact that Dometic never made anything like a "bet the company" move—often tempting when a business is on the ropes, but almost always a loser's game. As in the other cases of strategic renewal we studied, it redefined its core business by shifting its center of gravity along an existing vector of growth. To do this, it relied on hidden assets—resources or capabilities that it had not yet capitalized on. In Dometic's case, the treasure was its understanding of and access to customers in the RV market.

Leadership economics is a hallmark of almost every great strategy; when we see a situation in which the rich get richer, this is the phenomenon at work. Consider that most industries have more than six competitors, but usually more than 75% of the profit pool is captured by the top two. Of those two, the one with the greatest market power typically captures 70% of total profits and 75% of profits above the cost of capital. When Dometic focused on a defined market where it could stake out a leadership position, enormous financial benefits followed.

Its new growth formula offers the same kind of repeatability the old one did. Recall that Dometic's first focus was on applications for absorption refrigeration, which it pursued product by product, one of which was for RVs. The new formula angled off into a sequence of interior components for the RV customer base. Recently, as RV sales have slowed, Dometic has moved into interior systems for "live-in" vehicles in general, including boats and long-haul trucks.

Where Assets Hide

The importance of a company's overlooked, undervalued, or underutilized assets to its strategic regeneration cannot be overstated. In 21 of the 25 companies we examined, a hidden asset was the centerpiece of the new strategy.

Some of their stories are well known. A few years ago, a struggling Apple realized that its flair for software, user-friendly product design, and imaginative marketing could be applied to more than just computers—in particular, to a little device for listening to music. Today Apple's iPod-based music business accounts for nearly 50% of the company's revenues and 40% of profits—a new core. IBM's Global Services Group was once a tiny services and network-operations unit, not even a stand-alone business within IBM. By 2001 it was larger than all of IBM's hardware business and accounted for roughly two-thirds of the company's market value.

Why would well-established companies even have hidden assets? Shouldn't those assets have been put to work or disposed of long since? Actually, large, complex organizations always acquire more skills, capabilities, and business platforms than they can focus on at any one time. Some are necessarily neglected—and once they have been neglected for a while, a company's leaders often continue to ignore them or discount their value. But then something happens: Market conditions change, or perhaps the company acquires new capabilities that complement its forgotten ones. Suddenly the ugly ducklings in the backyard begin to look like swans in training.

The real question, then, is how to open management's eyes to the hidden assets in its midst. One way is to identify the richest hunting grounds. Our research suggests that hidden assets tend to fall into three categories: undervalued business platforms, untapped insights into customers, and underexploited capabilities. The exhibit "Where Does Your Future Lie?" details the types of assets we've seen exploited in each category. For a better understanding of how these assets came to light, let's look at some individual examples.

UNDERVALUED BUSINESS PLATFORMS

PerkinElmer was once the market leader in optical electronics for analytical instruments, such as spectrophotometers and gas chromatographs. Its optical capabilities were so strong that the company was chosen to manufacture the Hubble Space Telescope's mirrors and sighting equipment for NASA. Yet by 1993 PerkinElmer, its core product lines under attack by lower-cost and more innovative competitors, had stalled out. Revenues were stuck at $1.2 billion, exactly where they had been ten years earlier, and the market value of the company

---

Where Does Your Future Lie?

If the core of your business is nearing depletion, the temptation may be great to venture dramatically away from it—to rely on a major acquisition, for instance, in order to establish a foothold in a new, booming industry. But the history of corporate transformation shows you're more likely to be successful if you seek change in your own backyard.

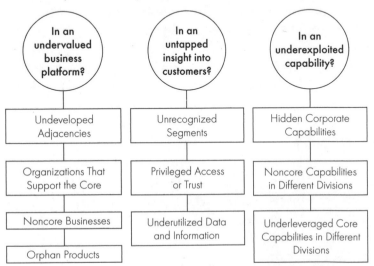

had eroded along with its earnings; the bottom line showed a loss of $83 million in 1993. In 1995 the board hired a new CEO, Tony White, to renew the company's strategy and performance and, if necessary, to completely redefine its core business.

As White examined the range of product lines and the customer segments served, he noticed a hidden asset that could rescue the company. In the early 1990s, PerkinElmer had branched out in another direction—developing products to amplify DNA—through a strategic alliance with Cetus Corporation. In the process, the company obtained rights to cutting-edge procedures known as polymerase chain reaction technology—a key life-sciences platform. In 1993, the company also acquired a small Silicon Valley life-sciences equipment company, Applied Biosystems (AB)—one more line of instruments to be integrated into PerkinElmer's.

White began to conceive of a redefined core built around analytical instruments for the fast-growing segment of life-sciences labs. The AB instruments in the company's catalog, if reorganized and given appropriate resources and direction, could have greater potential than even the original core. White says, "I was struck by how misconceived it was to tear AB apart and distribute its parts across the functions in the organization. I thought, 'Here is a company whose management does not see what they have.' So one of the first steps I took was to begin to reassemble the parts of AB. I appointed a new president of the division and announced that I was going to re-form the core of the company over a three-year period around this unique platform with leadership in key life-sciences detection technology."

Over the next three years, White and his team separated PerkinElmer's original core business and all the life-sciences products and services into two organizations. The employees in the analytical instruments division were given incentives to meet an aggressive cost reduction and cash flow target and told that the division would be spun off as a separate business or sold to a strong partner. Meanwhile, White set up a new data and diagnostics subsidiary, Celera Genomics, which, fueled by the passion of the scientist Craig Venter, famously went on to sequence the complete human genome. Celera and AB were combined into a new core business organization, a holding company christened Applera.

While Celera garnered the headlines, AB became the gold standard in the sequencing instrument business, with the leading market share. Today it has revenues of $1.9 billion and a healthy net income of $275 million. Meanwhile, the original instrument company was sold to the Massachusetts-based EG&G. (Soon after, EG&G changed its corporate name to PerkinElmer—and has since prospered from a combination that redefined its own core.)

The PerkinElmer-to-Applera transformation offers several lessons. The first is that a hidden asset may be a collection of products and customer relationships in different areas of a company that can be collected to form a new core. The second lesson is the power of market leadership: Finding a subcore of leadership buried in the company and building on it in a focused way created something that started smaller than the original combination but became much bigger and stronger. The third lesson lies in the concept of shrinking to grow. Though it sounds paradoxical and is organizationally difficult for companies to come to grips with, this is one of the most underused and underappreciated growth strategies. (See "Shrinking to Grow" at the end of this article.)

Creating a new core based on a previously overlooked business platform is more common than one might think. General Electric, for instance, like IBM, identified an internal business unit—GE Capital—that was under-valued and underutilized. Fueled by new attention and investment, the once sleepy division made more than 170 acquisitions over a ten-year period, propelling GE's growth. By 2005 GE Capital accounted for 35% of the parent corporation's profits. Nestlé discovered that it had a number of food and drink products designed to be consumed outside the home. Like the original PerkinElmer, it assembled these products into a new unit, Nestlé Food Services; developed a unified strategy; and effectively created the core of a new multibillion-dollar business.

UNTAPPED INSIGHTS INTO CUSTOMERS

Most large companies gather considerable amounts of data about the people and businesses that buy their wares. But it's not always clear how much they actually know about those customers. In a recent series of business seminars I held for management teams, the participants took an online survey. Though nearly all came from well-regarded companies, fewer than 25% agreed with the simple statement "We understand our customers." In a 2004 Bain survey, we asked respondents to identify the most important capabilities their companies could acquire to trigger a new wave of growth. "Capabilities to understand our core customers more deeply" topped the list.

For just this reason, insights into and relationships with customers are often hidden assets. A company may discover that one neglected customer segment holds the

key to unprecedented growth. It may find that it is in a
position of influence over its customers, perhaps because
of the trust and reputation it enjoys, and that it has not
fully developed this position. Or it may find that it has
proprietary data that can be used to alter, deepen, or
broaden its customer relationships. All these can stimu-
late growth around a new core.

Harman International, a maker of high-end audio
equipment, redefined its core around an unexploited
customer segment. In the early 1990s it was focused primarily on the consumer and professional audio markets,
with less than 10% of revenues coming from the original-
equipment automotive market. But its growth had stag-
nated and its profits were near zero. In 1993 Sidney Harman, a cofounder, who had left the company to serve as
U.S. deputy secretary of commerce, returned as CEO in
an attempt to rejuvenate the company.

Harman cast a curious eye on the automotive segment. He realized that people were spending more time
in their cars, and that many drivers were music lovers
accustomed to high-end equipment at home. Hoping to
beef up the company's sales in this sector, he acquired
the German company Becker, which supplied radios to
Mercedes-Benz. One day when Harman was visiting their
plant, some Becker engineers demonstrated how new
digital hardware allowed the company to create high-
performance audio equipment in a much smaller space
than before. That, Harman says, was the turning point.
He invested heavily in digital to create branded high-end
automotive "infotainment" systems. The systems proved
to have immense appeal both for car buyers and for car
manufacturers, who enjoyed healthy margins on the
equipment. Based largely on its success in the automotive market, Harman's market value increased 40-fold
from 1993 to 2005.

It is somewhat unusual, of course, to find an untapped customer segment that is poised for such rapid growth. But it isn't at all unusual for a company to discover that its relationships with customers are deeper than it realized, or that it has more knowledge about customers than it has put to work. Hyperion Solutions, a producer of financial software, was able to reinvent itself around new products and a new sales-and-service platform precisely because corporate finance departments had come to depend on its software for financial consolidation and SEC reporting. "We totally underestimated how much they relied upon us for this very technical and sensitive part of their job," says Jeff Rodek, formerly Hyperion's CEO and now the executive chairman. American Express transformed its credit-card business on the basis of previously unutilized knowledge of how different customer segments used the cards and what other products might appeal to them. Even De Beers, long known for its monopolistic practices in the diamond industry, recently redefined its core around consumer and customer relationships. De Beers, of course, had long-standing relationships with everyone in the industry. When its competitive landscape changed with the emergence of new rivals, De Beers leaders Nicky Oppenheimer and Gary Ralfe decided to make the company's strong brand and its unique image and relationships the basis of a major strategic redefinition. The company liquidated 80% of its inventory—the stockpile that had allowed it for so long to stabilize diamond prices—and created a new business model. It built up its brand through advertising. It developed new product ideas for its distributors and jewelers, and sponsored ad campaigns to market them to consumers. As a result, the estimated value of De Beers's diamond business increased nearly tenfold. The company is still in the business of selling rough diamonds, but its core is no longer about controlling supply—it's about serving consumers and customers.

UNDEREXPLOITED CAPABILITIES

Hidden business platforms and hidden customer insights are assets that companies already possess; in theory, all that remains is for management to uncover them and put them to work. Capabilities—the ability to perform specific tasks over and over again—are different. Any capability is potentially available to any company. What matters is how individual companies combine multiple capabilities into "activity systems," as Michael Porter calls them, meaning combinations of business processes that create hard-to-replicate competitive advantage. IKEA's successful business formula, Porter argued in his 1996 HBR article "What Is Strategy?" can be traced to a strong and unique set of linked capabilities, including global sourcing, design for assembly, logistics, and cost management.

An underexploited capability, therefore, can be an engine of growth if and only if it can combine with a company's other capabilities to produce something distinctly new and better. Consider the Danish company Novozymes, now a world leader in the development and production of high-quality enzymes. When it was spun off from its parent corporation in 2000, Novozymes was still largely dependent on relatively low-tech commodity enzymes such as those used in detergents.

Steen Riisgaard, the company's chief executive, set out to change that, and the key was Novozymes's underutilized scientific capability. Riisgaard focused the company's R&D on the creation of bioengineered specialty enzymes. Its scientists worked closely with customers in

order to design the enzymes precisely to their specifica-
tions. If a customer wanted to remove grease stains from
laundry at unusually low temperatures, for instance,
Novozymes would collect possible enzyme-producing
microorganisms from all over the world, determine
which one produced the enzyme closest to what was
needed, remove the relevant gene, and insert the gene
into an organism that could safely be produced at high
volume. Riisgaard likens the process to finding a needle
in a haystack, except that Novozymes uses state-of-the-
art technology to single out the haystacks and accelerate
the search. Such capabilities have shortened product
development from five years to two and have set
Novozymes apart from its competitors.

Of course, a company may find that it needs to
acquire new capabilities to complement those it already
has before it can create a potent activity system. Apple
indisputably capitalized on its strengths in design, brand
management, user interface, and elegant, easy-to-use
software in creating the iPod. But it also needed expertise in the music business and in digital rights management. Once it had those, Apple gained access to content
by signing up the top four recording companies before
competitors could and developing the iTunes Music
Store. It also created a brilliantly functional approach to
digital rights management with its Fairplay software,
which ensures that the music companies obtain a highly
controllable revenue stream. This combination of existing and new capabilities proved transformational for
Apple.

The highest form of capability development is to create a unique set of capabilities—no longer hidden—that
can build one growth platform after another, repeatedly
giving a company competitive advantage in multiple

markets. Though difficult, this is a strong temptation; indeed, it has proved to be a siren song for many. But a few companies, such as Emerson Electric, Valspar, Medtronic, and Johnson & Johnson, have managed to avoid the rocks. A lesser-known example is Danaher, which only 20 years ago was a midsize company with $617 million in revenues and almost all its business concentrated in industrial tool markets. Danaher developed a set of procedures whereby it can identify acquisitions and then add value to the acquired companies through the so-called Danaher Business System. The system has several phases and dimensions, including cultural values, productivity improvement, sourcing techniques, and a distinctive approach to measurement and control. It has allowed Danaher to expand into six strategic platforms and 102 subunits spanning a wide range of industrial applications, from electronic testing to environmental services. The company's stock price has risen by more than 5,000% since 1987, outpacing the broader market by a factor of more than five.

It's somewhat maddening how the assets explored here—PerkinElmer's undervalued business platform, Harman's untapped customer insights, Novozymes's underexploited capabilities—can be so obvious in hindsight and yet were so hard to appreciate at the time. Will you be any better able to see what is under your nose? One thing seems clear: Your next core business will not announce itself with fanfare. More likely, you will arrive at it by a painstaking audit of the areas outlined in this article.

The first step is simply to shine a light on the dark corners of your business and identify assets that are candidates for a new core. Once identified, these assets must be assessed. Do they offer the potential of clear, measurable differentiation from your competition? Can they provide tangible added value for your customers? Is there a robust profit pool that they can help you target? Can you acquire the additional capabilities you may need to implement the redefinition? Like the four essentials of a good golf swing, each of these requirements sounds easily met; the difficulty comes in meeting all four at once. Apple's iPod-based redefinition succeeded precisely because the company could answer every question in the affirmative. A negative answer to any one of them would have torpedoed the entire effort.

A Growing Imperative for Management

Learning to perform such assessments and to take gradual, confident steps toward a new core business is increasingly central to the conduct of corporate management. Look, for example, at the fate of the *Fortune* 500 companies in 1994. A research team at Bain found that a decade later 153 of those companies had either gone bankrupt or been acquired, and another 130 had engineered a fundamental shift in their core business strategy. In other words, nearly six out of ten faced serious threats to their survival or independence during the decade, and only about half of this group were able to meet the threat successfully by redefining their core business.

Why do so many companies face the need to transform themselves? Think of the cycle that long-lived companies commonly go through: They prosper first by focusing relentlessly on what they do well, next by expanding on that core to grow, and then, when the core has lost its relevance, by redefining themselves and focusing anew on a different core strength. It seems clear that this focus-expand-redefine cycle has accelerated over the decades. Companies move from one phase to another faster than they once did. The forces behind the acceleration are for the most part well known. New technologies lower costs and shorten product life cycles. New competitors—currently in China and India—shake up whole industries. Capital, innovation, and management talent flow more freely and more quickly around the globe. The churn caused by all this is wide-ranging. The average holding period for a share of common stock has declined from three years in the 1980s to nine months today. The average life span of companies has dropped from 14 years to just over ten, and the average tenure of CEOs has declined from eight years a decade ago to less than five today.

Business leaders are acutely aware of these waves of change and their ramifications. In 2004 my colleagues and I surveyed 259 senior executives around the world about the challenges they faced. More than 80% of them indicated that the productive lives of their strategies were getting shorter. Seventy-two percent believed that their leading competitor would be a different company in five years. Sixty-five percent believed that they would need to restructure the business model that served their primary customers. As the focus-expand-redefine cycle continues to pick up speed, each year will find more companies in that fateful third phase, where redefinition is essential. For most, the right way forward will lie in assets that are hidden from view—in neglected businesses, unused customer insights, and latent capabilities that, once harnessed, can propel new growth.

Shrinking to Grow

WHEN A COMPANY uncovers an underutilized source of leadership economics, sometimes the best response is to "double down" on its investment in that area. A bold version of this is actually shrinking to grow. Consider the example of Royal Vopak.

If you are not in the oil or chemicals business, you may not be familiar with Vopak, but it is the world leader in independent tank storage of bulk oil and chemicals, operating in 75 port locations from Rotterdam to Houston to Singapore. Vopak traces its roots back to a time when the Netherlands was the wealthiest and most powerful country in the world, owing to its role as a center for shipping and trade with the Far East. The origins of Vopak lie in a company that was founded in 1616, by a group of porters on the docks of Amsterdam, for the purpose of loading and unloading ship cargoes.

By 2000 Vopak was enjoying sales of €5.6 billion, with positions in shipping, chemical distribution, and port storage facilities. Its storage business was the most profitable. When Vopak's profits suffered and its stock price came under severe pressure, plummeting from €25 per share in June 1999 to €12 in July 2002, the company took decisive action. It spun off everything but the storage business, reducing the sales volume of the company to €750 million. But Vopak did not stop there: It even sold some of its storage portfolio, further reducing its size.

What was the result? Amazingly, the company's market value increased beyond its original level, as the stock price rebounded to €30 in May 2006. Furthermore, the

stronger, well-funded business began to grow again—
both organically and through acquisitions and new port
locations. During the first half of 2006, Vopak's revenues
grew by 17% and its earnings by 28%, in an inherently
low-growth industry. John Paul Broeders, the chairman of
the executive board, says, "Without shrinking first, we
would never have created the resources, the management focus, and a stable platform to begin to grow
again as we have."

Shrink-to-grow strategies are not an end in themselves, but they can pave the way for redefinition. These
moves have a very high success rate when it comes to
increasing a company's value and liberating one of the
cores to strengthen and grow, provided it's given additional resources. Indeed, another three of our 25 case
studies in successful core redefinition relied on this tactic:
PerkinElmer, Samsung, and GUS.

Seven Steps to a New Core Business

1. Define the core of your business. Reach consensus on
   the true state of the core.

2. Assess the core's full potential and the durability of its key
   differentiation.

3. Develop a point of view about the future, and define the
   status quo.

4. Identify the full range of options for redefining the core
   from the inside and from the outside.

5. Identify your hidden assets, and ask whether they create
   new options or enable others.

6. Use key criteria (leadership, profit pool, repeatability, chances of implementation) in deciding which assets to employ in redefining your core.

7. Set up a program office to help initiate, track, and manage course corrections.

Originally published in April 2007
Reprint R0704D

Leading Change When Business Is Good

An Interview with
Samuel J. Palmisano

PAUL HEMP AND THOMAS A. STEWART

Executive Summary

LOU GERSTNER'S was a hard act to follow. As CEO in what were arguably IBM's darkest hours, Gerstner brought the company back from the brink. After nearly ten wrenching years, in which the big-machine manufacturer remade itself into a comprehensive software, hardware, and services provider, business was looking good. So the challenge for Sam Palmisano, when he took over as CEO in 2002, was to come up with a mandate for a second act in the company's transformation.

His primary aim was to get different parts of the company working together so IBM could offer customers "integrated solutions"—hardware, software, services, and financing—at a single price. As part of this effort, he asked all of IBM's 320,000 employees, in 170 countries, to weigh in on a new set of shared corporate values.

Over a 72-hour period, thousands of IBMers throughout the world gave Palmisano and his executive team an earful in an intranet discussion dubbed "Values-Jam," an often-heated debate about the company's heart and soul. Twenty-four hours into the exercise, at least one senior exec wanted to pull the plug. The jam had clearly struck a chord with employees, but it was a dissonant one, full of rancor and discontent.

Palmisano let the discussion continue, and the next day, the mood began to shift. The criticism became more constructive. Out of the million words generated by the jam grew a set of values that, as Palmisano explains in this interview, are meant to guide the operational decisions made by IBM's employees—and, more important, to serve as Palmisano's mandate to continue the reinvention of the company.

In July 2003, International Business Machines Corporation conducted a 72-hour experiment whose outcome was as uncertain as anything going on in its research labs. Six months into a top-to-bottom review of its management organization, IBM held a three-day discussion via the corporate intranet about the company's values. The forum, dubbed ValuesJam, joined thousands of employees in a debate about the very nature of the computer giant and what it stood for.

Over the three days, an estimated 50,000 of IBM's employees—including CEO Sam Palmisano—checked out the discussion, posting nearly 10,000 comments about the proposed values. The jam had clearly struck a chord.

But it was a disturbingly dissonant one. Some comments were merely cynical. One had the subject line:

"The only value in IBM today is the stock price."
Another read, "Company values (ya right)." Others,
though, addressed fundamental management issues. "I
feel we talk a lot about trust and taking risks. But at the
same time, we have endless audits, mistakes are punished and not seen as a welcome part of learning, and
managers (and others) are consistently checked," wrote
one employee. "There appears to be a great reluc-
tance among our junior executive community to challenge the views of our senior execs," said another.
"Many times I have heard expressions like, 'Would you
tell Sam that his strategy is wrong!!?' " Twenty-four hours
into the exercise, at least one senior executive wanted
to pull the plug.

But Palmisano wouldn't hear of it. And then the mood
began to shift. After a day marked by critics letting off
steam, the countercritics began to weigh in. While
acknowledging the company's shortcomings, they
argued that much of IBM's culture and values was worth
preserving. "Shortly after joining IBM 18 years ago,"
wrote one, "I was asked to serve on a jury. When I
approached the bench and answered [the lawyers']
questions, I was surprised when the judge said, 'You
guys can pick whoever else you want, but I want this
IBMer on that jury.' I have never felt so much pride. His
statement said it all: integrity, excellence, and quality."
Comments like these became more frequent, criticism
became more constructive, and the ValuesJam conversation stabilized.

The question of what was worth preserving and what
needed to be changed was at the heart of ValuesJam. In
1914—when the company was making tabulating
machines, scales for weighing meat, and cheese slicers—
president Thomas Watson, Sr., decreed three corporate

principles, called the Basic Beliefs: "respect for the individual," "the best customer service," and "the pursuit of excellence." They would inform IBM's culture, and help drive its success, for more than half a century.

By 2002, when Palmisano took over as CEO, much had happened to Big Blue. In the early 1990s, the company had suffered the worst reversal in its history and then, under Lou Gerstner, had fought its way back, transformed from a mainframe maker into a robust provider of integrated hardware, networking, and software solutions. Palmisano felt that the Basic Beliefs could still serve the company—but now as the foundation for a new set of corporate values that could energize employees even more than its near-death experience had. Looking for a modern-day equivalent, Palmisano first queried 300 of his senior executives, then quickly opened up the discussion, through a survey of over a thousand employees, to get a sense of how people at all levels, functions, and locations would articulate IBM's values and their aspirations for the company. Out of this research grew the propositions that were debated in ValuesJam.

After—and even during—the jam, company analysts pored over the postings, mining the million-word text for key themes. Finally, a small team that included Palmisano came up with a revised set of corporate values. The CEO announced the new values to employees in an intranet broadcast in November 2003: "dedication to every client's success," "innovation that matters—for our company and for the world," "trust and personal responsibility in all relationships." Earthshaking? No, but imbued with legitimacy and packed with meaning and implications for IBM.

To prove that the new values were more than window dressing, Palmisano immediately made some changes. He called on the director of a major business unit—e-business hosting services for the U.S. industrial sector—and charged her with identifying gaps between the values and company practices. He bluntly told his 15 direct reports that they had better follow suit. Another online jam was held in October 2004 (this one informally dubbed a "logjam") in which employees were asked to identify organizational barriers to innovation and revenue growth.

Although Palmisano, by his own account, is building on a strategy laid down by Gerstner, the leadership styles of the two men are very different. Under Gerstner, there was little expansive talk about IBM's heritage. He was an outsider, a former CEO of RJR Nabisco and an ex-McKinsey consultant, who was faced with the daunting task of righting a sinking ship. In fact, he famously observed, shortly after taking over, that "the last thing IBM needs right now is a vision." Palmisano, by contrast, is a true-blue IBMer, who started at the company in 1973 as a salesman in Baltimore. Like many of his generation who felt such acute shame when IBM was brought to its knees in the early 1990s, he clearly has a visceral attachment to the firm—and to the hope that it may someday regain its former greatness. At the same time, the erstwhile salesman is, in the words of a colleague, "a results-driven, make-it-rain, close-the-deal sort of guy": not the first person you'd expect to hold forth on a subjective topic like "trust."

In this edited conversation with HBR senior editor Paul Hemp and HBR's editor, Thomas A. Stewart, Palmisano talks about the strategic importance of values to IBM. He

begins by explaining why—and how—hard financial met-
rics and soft corporate values can coexist.

Corporate values generally are feel-good statements
that have almost no effect on a company's operations.
What made—what makes—you think they can be more
than this?

Look at the portrait of Tom Watson, Sr., in our lobby.
You've never seen such a stern man. The eyes in the
painting stare right through you. This was *not* a soft individual. He was a capitalist. He wanted IBM to make
money, lots of it. But he was perceptive enough to build
the company in a way that would ensure its prosperity
long after he left the scene. His three Basic Beliefs successfully steered this company through persistent
change and repeated reinvention for more than 50 years.

An organic system, which is what a company is, needs
to adapt. And we think values—that's what we call them
today at IBM, but you can call them "beliefs" or "principles" or "precepts" or even "DNA"—are what enable you
to do that. They let you change everything, from your
products to your strategies to your business model, but
remain true to your essence, your basic mission and
identity.

Unfortunately, over the decades, Watson's Basic
Beliefs became distorted and took on a life of their own.
"Respect for the individual" became entitlement: not fair
work for all, not a chance to speak out, but a guaranteed
job and culture-dictated promotions. "The pursuit of
excellence" became arrogance: We stopped listening to
our markets, to our customers, to each other. We were so
successful for so long that we could never see another

point of view. And when the market shifted, we almost
went out of business. We had to cut a workforce of more
than 400,000 people in half. Over the course of several
years, we wiped out the equivalent of a medium-sized
northeastern city—say, Providence, Rhode Island.

If you lived through this, as I did, it was easy to see
how the company's values had become part of the problem. But I believe values can once again help guide us
through major change and meet some of the formidable
challenges we face.

For instance, I feel that a strong value system is crucial to bringing together and motivating a workforce as
large and diverse as ours has become. We have nearly
one-third of a million employees serving clients in 170
countries. Forty percent of those people don't report
daily to an IBM site; they work on the client's premises,
from home, or they're mobile. And, perhaps most significant, given IBM's tradition of hiring and training young
people for a lifetime of work, half of today's employees
have been with the company for fewer than five years
because of recent acquisitions and our relatively new
practice of hiring seasoned professionals. In a modest
hiring year, we now add 20,000 to 25,000 people.

*In effect, gradually repopulating Providence, Rhode
Island!*

Exactly. So how do you channel this diverse and constantly changing array of talent and experience into a
common purpose? How do you get people to *passion-
ately* pursue that purpose?

You could employ all kinds of traditional, top-down
management processes. But they wouldn't work at
IBM—or, I would argue, at an increasing number of

twenty-first-century companies. You just can't impose command-and-control mechanisms on a large, highly professional workforce. I'm not only talking about our scientists, engineers, and consultants. More than 200,000 of our employees have college degrees. The CEO can't say to them, "Get in line and follow me." Or "*I've* decided what *your* values are." They're too smart for that. And as you know, smarter people tend to be, well, a little more challenging; you might even say cynical.

But even if our people did accept this kind of traditional, hierarchical management system, our clients wouldn't. As we learned at IBM over the years, a top-down system can create a smothering bureaucracy that doesn't allow for the speed, the flexibility, the innovation that clients expect today.

So you're saying that values are about how employees behave when management isn't there, which it can't be—which it shouldn't be—given IBM's size and the need for people to make decisions quickly. You're basically talking about using values to manage.

Yes. A values-based management system. Let me cast the issue in a slightly different light. When you think about it, there's no optimal way to organize IBM. We traditionally were viewed as a large, successful, "well-managed" company. That was a compliment. But in today's fast-changing environment, it's a problem. You can easily end up with a bureaucracy of people overanalyzing problems and slowing down the decision-making process.

Think of our organizational matrix. Remember, we operate in 170 countries. To keep it simple, let's say we have 60 or 70 major product lines. We have more than a dozen customer segments. Well, if you mapped out the entire 3-D matrix, you'd get more than 100,000 cells— cells in which you have to close out P&Ls every day, make decisions, allocate resources, make trade-offs. You'll drive people crazy trying to centrally manage every one of those intersections.

So if there's no way to optimize IBM through organizational structure or by management dictate, you have to empower people while ensuring that they're making the right calls the right way. And by "right," I'm not talking about ethics and legal compliance alone; those are table stakes. I'm talking about decisions that support and give life to IBM's strategy and brand, decisions that shape a culture. That's why values, for us, aren't soft. They're the basis of what we do, our mission as a company. They're a touchstone for decentralized decision making. It used to be a rule of thumb that "people don't do what you expect; they do what you inspect." My point is that it's just not possible to inspect everyone anymore. But you also can't just let go of the reins and let people do what they want without guidance or context. You've got to create a management system that empowers people and provides a basis for decision making that is consistent with who we are at IBM.

How do the new values help further IBM's strategy?

In two main ways. Back some 12 years ago, three-fifths of our business was in computer hardware and roughly two-fifths was in software and services. Today, those numbers are more than reversed. Well, if three-fifths of your business is manufacturing, management is basically supervisory: "You do this. You do that." But that no longer works when your business is primarily based on knowledge. And your business model also changes dramatically.

For one thing, people—rather than products—become your brand. Just as our products have had to be consistent with the IBM brand promise, now more than ever, so do our people. One way to ensure that is to inform their behavior with a globally consistent set of values.

Second, the IT industry has continued to shift toward reintegration. We all know the story of how the industry fragmented in the 1980s and 1990s, with separate companies selling the processors, the storage devices, and the software that make up a computer system—almost killing IBM, the original vertically integrated computer company. Now customers are demanding a package of computer products and services from a single company, a company that can offer them an integrated solution to their business problems. This is a big opportunity for IBM. We probably have a wider array of computer products and services and know-how than anyone. But it's also a challenge. How can we get our people in far-flung business units with different financial targets and incentives working together in teams that can offer at a single price a comprehensive and customized solution—one that doesn't show the organizational seams?

Companies usually face the issue of workforce integration after a huge merger. We needed to integrate our existing workforce as a strategic response to the reintegration of the industry. It won't surprise you that I didn't think the answer lay in a new organizational structure or in more management oversight. What you need to foster this sort of cooperation is a common set of guidelines about how we make decisions, day in and day out. In other words, values.

And what happens when the strategy changes?

Ah, that's why the right set of values is so important. There's always going to be another strategy on the horizon as the market changes, as technologies come and go. So we wanted values that would foster an organization able to quickly execute a new strategy. At the same time, we wanted values that, like Watson's Basic Beliefs, would be enduring, that would guide the company through economic cycles and geopolitical shifts, that would transcend changes in products, technologies, employees, and leaders.

How did IBM distill new values from its past traditions and current employee feedback?

The last time IBM examined its values was nearly a century ago. Watson was an entrepreneur, leading what was, in today's lingo, a start-up. So in 1914, he simply said, "Here are our beliefs. Learn them. Live them." That was appropriate for his day, and there's no question it worked. But 90 years later, we couldn't have someone in headquarters sitting up in bed in the middle of the night and saying, "Here are our new values!" We couldn't be casual about tinkering with the DNA of a company like IBM. We had to come up with a way to get the employees to create the value system, to determine the company's principles. Watson's Basic Beliefs, however distorted they might have become over the years, had to be the starting point.

After getting input from IBM's top 300 executives and conducting focus groups with more than a thousand employees—a statistically representative cross-section—we came up with three perfectly sound values. [For a detailed description of how IBM got from the Basic

Beliefs to its new set of values, see "Continuity and Change" at the end of this article.] But I knew we'd eventually throw out the statements to everyone in the company to debate. That's where ValuesJam came in—this live, companywide conversation on our intranet.

What was your own experience during the jam? Did you have the feeling you'd opened Pandora's box?

I logged in from China. I was pretty jet-lagged and couldn't sleep, so I jumped in with postings on a lot of stuff, particularly around client issues. [For a selection of Palmisano's postings during the ValuesJam, see "Sam Joins the Fray" at the end of this article.] And yes, the electronic argument was hot and contentious and messy. But you had to get comfortable with that. Understand, we had done three or four big online jams before this, so we had some idea of how lively they can be. Even so, none of those could have prepared us for the emotions unleashed by this topic.

You had to put your ego aside—not easy for a CEO to do—and realize that this was the best thing that could have happened. You could say, "Oh my God, I've unleashed this incredible negative energy." Or you could say, "Oh my God, I now have this incredible mandate to drive even more change in the company."

When Lou Gerstner came here in 1993, there was clearly a burning platform. In fact, the whole place was in flames. There was even talk of breaking up the company. And he responded brilliantly. Here's this outsider who managed to marshal the collective urgency of tens of thousands of people like me to save this company and turn it around: without a doubt one of the greatest saves in business history. But the trick then wasn't creating a sense of urgency—we had that. Maybe you needed to

shake people out of being shell-shocked. But most
IBMers were willing to do whatever it took to save the
company, not to mention their own jobs. And there was
a lot of pride at stake. Lou's task was mostly to convince
people that he was making the right changes.

Once things got better, though, there was another
kind of danger: that we would slip back into complacency. As our financial results improved dramatically
and we began outperforming our competitors, people—
already weary from nearly a decade of change—would
say, "Well, why do I have to do things differently now?
The leadership may be different, but the strategy is fundamentally sound. Why do I have to change?" This is, by
the way, a problem that everyone running a successful
company wrestles with.

So the challenge shifted. Instead of galvanizing people
through fear of failure, you have to galvanize them
through hope and aspiration. You lay out the opportunity to become a great company again—the greatest in
the world, which is what IBM used to be. And you hope
people feel the same need, the urgency you do, to get
there. Well, I think IBMers today do feel that urgency.
Maybe the jam's greatest contribution was to make that
fact unambiguously clear to all of us, very visibly, in
public.

What were the chief points of debate—or contention?

There was actually remarkable agreement on *what* we all
value. The debate, as it turned out, wasn't over the values
themselves so much. The debate was about whether IBM
today is willing and able to live them.

For instance, people seemed to understand the need
to reintegrate the company, but there were complaints—
legitimate complaints—about things that are getting in

the way. People would describe extremely frustrating situations. They'd say something like: "I'm in Tokyo, prototyping software for a client, and I need a software engineer based in Austin *right now* to help in a blade server configuration. But I can't just say, 'Please come to Tokyo and help.' I need to get a charge code first so I can pay his department for his time!"

There's a collective impatience that we've been tapping into to drive the change needed to make IBM everything that all of us aspire for it to be. I'm convinced that we wouldn't have gotten to this point if we hadn't found a way to engage the entire IBM population in a genuine, candid conversation.

By the way, having a global, universally accessible intranet like ours certainly helps, but the technology isn't the point. I think we would've found a way to have this company-wide dialogue if the Web didn't exist. [For an explanation of how the jam worked, see "Managing ValuesJam" at the end of this article.]

What happened after the jam?

Well, we got a mountain of employee comments. The team analyzed all of it, and it was clear that the proposed value statements needed to change to reflect some of the nuances and emotion people expressed. So, drawing on this analysis, along with other employee feedback, a small team settled on IBM's new corporate values.

The first value is "dedication to every client's success." At one level, that's pretty straightforward: Bring together all of IBM's capability—in the laboratory, in the field, in the back office, wherever—to help solve difficult problems clients can't solve themselves. But this is also a lot more than the familiar claim of unstinting customer service. "Client success" isn't just "the customer is always right." It means maintaining a long-term relationship where what happens after the deal is more important than what happens before it's signed. It means a persistent focus on outcomes. It means having skin in the game of your client's success, up to and including how your contracts are structured and what triggers your getting paid.

The second is "innovation that matters—for our company and for the world." When employees talked about IBM making a difference in the world, they included more than our work of inventing and building great products. They talked about how their work touches people and society, how we can help save lives—say, through our cutting-edge work with the Mayo Clinic or by helping governments fight terrorism with our data technology. This kind of innovation is a major reason we are able to attract great scientists. They can do cool stuff and maybe make more money in Silicon Valley—for a while, anyway—but they can do work that actually changes business and society at IBM. And it's also about what I mentioned before: a continually experimental attitude toward IBM itself. Over most of our 90 years, with the exception of that one period when we became arrogant and complacent, this company never stopped questioning assumptions, trying out different models, testing the limits—whether in technology or business or in progressive workforce policies. Employees reminded us that those things are innovations that matter at least as much as new products.

The third value is "trust and personal responsibility in all relationships." There's a lot in that statement, too. Interestingly, the feedback from employees on this value has focused on relationships among people at IBM. But we're also talking about the company's relationships with suppliers, with investors, with governments, with communities.

We published the values in their final form—along with some elaboration on them and some direct employee postings from the jam—in November 2003. Over the next ten days, more than 200,000 people downloaded the online document. The responses just flooded in, both in the form of postings on the intranet and in more than a thousand e-mails sent directly to me, telling us in often sharp language just where IBM's operations fell short of, or clashed with, these ideals. Some of the comments were painful to read. But, again, they exhibited something every leader should welcome: People here aren't complacent about the company's future. And the comments were, by and large, extremely thoughtful.

What did you do with this feedback?

We collected and collated it. Then I printed all of it out— the stack of paper was about three feet high—and took it home to read over one weekend. On Monday morning, I walked into our executive committee meeting and threw it on the table. I said, "You guys ought to read every one of these comments, because if you think we've got this place plumbed correctly, think again."

Don't get me wrong. The passion in these e-mails was positive as well as negative. People would say, literally, "I'm weeping. These values describe the company I joined, the company I believe in. We can truly make this place great again. But we've got all these things in our way. . . ." The raw emotion of some of the e-mails was really something.

Now, if you've unleashed all this frustration and energy, if you've invited people to feel hope about something they really care about, you'd better be prepared to do something in response. So, in the months since we finalized the values, we've announced some initiatives that begin to close the gaps.

One I have dubbed our "$100 million bet on trust." We kept hearing about situations like our colleague in Tokyo who needed help from the engineer in Austin, cases in which employees were unable to respond quickly to client needs because of financial control processes that required several levels of management approval. The money would usually be approved, but too late. So we allocated managers up to $5,000 annually they could spend, no questions asked, to respond to extraordinary situations that would help generate business or develop client relationships or to respond to an IBMer's emergency need. We ran a pilot for a few months with our 700 client-facing teams, and they spent the money intelligently. There were lots of examples of teams winning deals and delighting clients with a small amount of "walk around money" to spend at their discretion. So, based on the success of that pilot, we expanded the program to all 22,000 IBM first-line managers.

You can do the math: $5,000 times 22,000 managers is a big number. I'm sure there were people in the company who said, "We need to get this under control." But they're not the CEO. Yes, you need financial controls. Yes, not every dollar spent from this Managers' Value Fund will yield some tangible return. But I'm confident that allowing line managers to take some reasonable risks, and trusting them with those decisions, will pay off over time. The program also makes a point: that we live by our values.

The value of "trust and personal responsibility in all relationships"—including those with IBM's shareholders—led to another initiative: a change in the way we grant top executive stock options. After getting a lot of outside experts to study this (and concluding that the complicated algorithms they recommended were wonderful, if you wanted to hire the outsiders as permanent consultants, but terrible if you wanted a simple formula that aligned executive behavior with shareholder interests), we settled on a straightforward idea. Senior executives will benefit from their options only after shareholders have realized at least 10% growth in their investments—that is, the strike price is 10% higher than the market price on the day the options are issued. Look at it this way: IBM's market value would have to increase by $17 billion from that date before any of the execs realize a penny of benefit. We think we are the first large company to take such a radical step—and it grew out of our values.

Let me give you one more example. It may not sound like a big deal, but for us, it was radical. We overhauled the way we set prices. We heard time and again from employees about how difficult it was to put together a client-friendly, cross-IBM solution, one involving a variety of products and services at a single, all-inclusive price. We couldn't do it. Every brand unit had its own P&L, and all the people who determine prices had been organized by brand. Remember those 100,000 cells in our 3-D matrix? Our people were pulling their cross-IBM bids apart, running them through our financial-accounting system as separate bids for individual products and services. This was nuts, because it's our ability to offer everything—hardware, software, services, and financing—that gives us a real advantage. When we bid on each of the parts separately, we go head-to-head against rivals by product: EMC in storage, say, or Accenture in services. This was tearing out the very heart of our strategy of integration, not to mention our unique kind of business-plus-technology innovation.

Let me give you a humorous (if somewhat discouraging) illustration. Every senior executive has responsibility for at least one major client—we call them "partnership accounts." Our former CFO John Joyce, who now heads IBM's services business, put together a deal for his account that involved some hardware, some software, and some services. He was told he couldn't price it as an integrated solution. And he's the CFO! So we figured out a way to set a single price for each integrated offering.

This sounds like a great business move. But what does it have to do with values? Wouldn't you ultimately have decided you had to do that in any case?

To be honest, we'd been debating the pricing issue at the executive level for a long time. But we hadn't done anything about it. The values initiative forced us to confront the issue, and it gave us the impetus to make the change. You know, there are always ingrained operations and habits of mind in any organization—I don't care whether it's a business or a university or a government. Well, the values and the jam were great inertia-busting vehicles. A small business in this place is $15 billion, and a big one is $40 billion. So you have senior vice presidents running *Fortune* 500–sized companies who aren't necessarily looking for bright ideas from the CEO or some task force every day. But when you hear from so many of our people on the front lines, you can't just ignore it. They're crying out: "We say we value 'client success,' and we want to grow our business. This one thing is getting in the way of both!" You've got to pay attention—if not to me, then to them.

So we took the pricers—the people who set the prices for client bids—and we said to them, "You work for IBM. When there's a cross-IBM bid with multiple products, you price it on the IBM income statement, not on the income statements of each product." Needless to say, this involved a series of very difficult meetings with senior executives. There was a huge debate among the finance people about all the reasons why we couldn't do it: "It will be too much work to reallocate all the costs and revenue of a project back to individual profit centers." And they're right: It isn't easy, especially when we now have to certify everything. But the CFO was with me on this: After all, he'd seen the problem firsthand! And we made the change, so that now when we make a truly cross-IBM bid, we can optimize it for the client and for us.

This brings us back to the tension between soft values and hard financial metrics. In the long run, they shouldn't conflict. But along the way, they're going to be jabbing at each other. After all, people still have to make their numbers.

Certainly, there's no getting around that in a commercial enterprise. But I think values inject balance in the company's culture and management system: balance between the short-term transaction and the long-term relationship, balance between the interests of shareholders, employees, and clients. In every case, you have to make a call. Values help you make those decisions, not on an ad hoc basis, but in a way that is consistent with your culture and brand, with who you are as a company.

Look at how we compensate our managing directors, who are responsible for our largest client relationships. We decided to take half their comp and calculate it not on an annual basis but on a rolling three-year basis. We ask clients to score the managing director's performance at the end of a project or engagement, which might last longer than a single year, and that plays a big part in his bonus. So a big piece of his compensation is based on a combination of the project's profitability—whether the manager made his annual numbers—and on the client's satisfaction over a longer-term horizon. The managing director can't trade off one for the other.

So we've tried to keep balance in the system, to make sure that things aren't completely oriented toward short-term financials. But you're absolutely right: There are times when people will argue, "Well, jeez, you guys are pushing us in both directions." It's a valid debate. I think, though, that the best place to have that debate is at the lowest level of your organization, because that's where these decisions are being made and having an impact. Thousands of these interactions go on every day that none of us at the top will ever, or should ever, know about. But you hope that the values are providing a counterweight to the drive for short-term profitability in all those interactions. In the long term, I think, whether or not you have a values-driven culture is what makes you a winner or a loser.

You've had the new values in place for just about a year now. They've already created strong emotions and high expectations. What's the prognosis?

We're just starting down the road on what is probably a ten- to 15-year process. I was back in Asia not long ago, and I did one of these town hall–style meetings with IBM employees and talked about the values. Probably two-thirds of the people clearly knew about them, had read

about them. But a third of the people—you could look at
their faces and see it—hadn't even heard of the values.
Or at least the values hadn't resonated with them yet. So
we have work to do. Not just in getting everyone to mem-
orize three pithy statements. We need to do a heck of a
lot to close the gaps between our stated values and the
reality of IBM today. That's the point of it all.

I know that not everyone on my executive team is as
enthusiastic about the values initiative as I am—though
they'd never admit it! But people on the senior team who
lived through IBM's near-death experience will do anything not to go back to that. The blow to everyone's pride
when IBM became the laughingstock of the business
world was almost too much to bear. I have zero resis-
tance from the senior team to initiatives that can save us
from a return to that. And our values work is one of the
most important of those initiatives.

Then look at the employee response to ValuesJam.
There is an unmistakable yearning for this to be a great
company. I mean, why have people joined IBM over the
years? There are a lot of places to make money, if that's
what drives you. Why come here?

I believe it's because they want to be part of a progressive company that makes a difference in the world. They
want to be in the kind of company that supports
research that wins Nobel Prizes, that changes the way
people think about business itself, that is willing to take
firm positions on unpopular issues based on principle.

You know, back in the 1950s, Watson, Jr., wrote the
governors of southern states that IBM would not adhere
to separate-but-equal laws, and then the company codi-
fied an equal-opportunity policy years before it was man-
dated by law. I've got to believe that a company that con-
ceives of itself that way, and that seriously manages itself

accordingly, has strong appeal to a lot of people. We can't offer them the promise of instant wealth, which they may get at a start-up, or a job for life, as in the old days. But we can offer them something worth believing in and working toward.

If we get most people in this company excited about that, they're going to pull the rest of the company with them. If they become dedicated to these values and what we're trying to accomplish, I can go to sleep at night confident of our future.

Continuity and Change

IBM'S NEW VALUES grew out of a long tradition. In 1914, Thomas Watson, Sr., the founder of the modern International Business Machines Corporation, laid out three principles known as the *Basic Beliefs:*

- Respect for the individual
- The best customer service
- The pursuit of excellence

Although these beliefs played a significant role in driving IBM's success over most of the twentieth century, they eventually were subsumed—and, in effect, redefined—by a sense of entitlement and arrogance within the organization. That, according to CEO Sam Palmisano, contributed to the company's failure to respond to market changes in the early 1990s and to its near demise.

In February 2003, just under a year after taking over as CEO, at a meeting of IBM's top 300 managers, Palmisano raised the idea of reinventing the company's values as a way to manage and reintegrate the sprawling and diverse enterprise. He put forth *four concepts,* three of them drawn from Watson's Basic Beliefs, as possible bases for the new values:

- Respect
- Customer
- Excellence
- Innovation

These were "test marketed" through surveys and focus groups with more than 1,000 IBM employees. The notion of "respect" was thrown out because of its connotations of the past. It was also decided that statements rather than just words would be more compelling.

Out of this process grew the three *proposed values* discussed during the July 2003 online forum, ValuesJam:

- Commitment to the customer
- Excellence through innovation
- Integrity that earns trust

Using a specially tailored "jamalyzer" tool—based on IBM's e-classifier software, but turbocharged with additional capabilities designed to process constantly changing content—IBM analysts crunched the million-plus words posted during the ValuesJam. Some themes emerged. For example, many people said that a silo mentality pitted the business units against one another, to the detriment of IBM as a whole. Several people characterized this as a trust issue. But the proposed value "integrity that earns trust" was criticized as being too vague. Some thought it was just another way of saying "respect for the individual," one of the original Basic Beliefs that many now viewed as outdated. And the

notion of trust was seen as being too inwardly focused—
management trusting its employees—and not prescriptive
enough in terms of how employees should behave with
each other or with parties outside the company.

Drawing on this analysis, the results of pre- and post-
jam surveys, and a full reading of the raw transcripts, a
small team, with input from Palmisano, arrived at a
revised set of *new corporate values*:

- Dedication to every client's success
- Innovation that matters—for our company and for the world
- Trust and personal responsibility in all relationships

These were published on the company intranet in
November 2003.

Sam Joins the Fray

IBM CEO SAM PALMISANO was in China on business
during ValuesJam, and he logged on from there. Following are some of his comments (typos included) on a number of topics raised by employees during the online
forum:

YES, values matter!!!!! (6 reply)
Samuel J. Palmisano 29 Jul 2003 20:00 GMT

Good discussion about the need for values/princi-
ples/belifes, etc. people can be very cynical and sar-
castic about this kind of topic, but I appreciate the
thoughtful constructive comments I'm seeing. Personaly, I
believe "values" should embrace a company's broader
role in the world—with customers, society, culture, etc.—as

well as how its people work together.. I hope this Jam elevates IBMs ambitions about its mission in the 21st century.. WE have a unique opprtunity for IBM to set the pace for ALL companies, not just the techs.

doing the right thing for customers . . . (21 reply)

Samuel J. Palmisano 29 Jul 2003 20:07 GMT

Early in my career when I was in the field in Baltimore, one of our systems failed for a healthcare customer. The customer went to manual processes, but said they would start losing patients within hours if the system couldnt be fixed. The branch mgr called one of our competitors and orderd another system. so two teams of IBMERS worked side by side..one to fix the system, the others to bring up the new one. the mgr never asked Hq what to do.. it was a great lesson in how far this company will go to help a customer in time of need. btw, we fixed the system in time.

integrity/trust in ALL our relationships matter!!!! (44 reply)

Samuel J. Palmisano 29 Jul 2003 20:12 GMT

very interesting discussion . . . one thing I'm noticing, and it was in the broadcast feedback too: not too many of you are talking about integrity and trust when it comes to our OTHER relationships that are key to IBMs success—customers, communities where we live, owners of the company etc. any thoghts on why thats so? maybe we're too inwardly focused?

a world without IBM???? (35 reply)

Samuel J. Palmisano 29 Jul 2003 20:20 GMT

No IBM? the industry would stop growing because no one would invent anything that ran for more than

THREE MINUTES..no IBM means no grownups . . . no IBM means no truly global company that brings economic growth, respect progress to societies everywhere . . . no IBM means no place to work for hundreds of thousands of people who want more than a job, they want to ,MAKE A DIFFERENCE in the world.

suggestion for Sam (9 reply)

Samuel J. Palmisano 29 Jul 2003 20:25 GMT
   steve, you make good points about how/when we win . . . we can blow up more burecracy if we all behave like mature adutls and take into account ALL OF THE INTERESTS of IBm FIRST..customers, employees, shareholders, doing whats right for the LONG TERM intersts of the company. mgrs have an importrant role to play in encouraing this kind of behavior . . . you have my support.

Managing ValuesJam

IBM HAD EXPERIMENTED before with jam sessions—relatively unstructured employee discussions around broad topics—both on the corporate intranet and in face-to-face off-site brainstorming sessions. But the 72-hour ValuesJam, held in July 2003, was the most ambitious, focusing as it did on the very nature and future of IBM.

One thing was clear: You wouldn't be able to orchestrate a forum like this, the verbal equivalent of an improvisational jam session among jazz musicians. In the words of CEO Sam Palmisano, "It just took off." But, much like a musical jam, the dialogue was informed by a number of themes:

Forum 1. Company Values

Do company values exist? If so, what is involved in establishing them? Most companies today have values statements. But what would a company look and act like that truly lived its beliefs? Is it important for IBM to agree on a set of lasting values that drive everything it does?

Forum 2. A First Draft

What values are essential to what IBM needs to become? Consider this list: 1. Commitment to the customer. 2. Excellence through innovation. 3. Integrity that earns trust. How might these values change the way we act or the decisions we make? Is there some important aspect or nuance that is missing?

Forum 3. A Company's Impact

If our company disappeared tonight, how different would the world be tomorrow? Is there something about our company that makes a unique contribution to the world?

Forum 4. The Gold Standard

When is IBM at its best? When have you been proudest to be an IBMer? What happened, and what was uniquely meaningful about it? And what do we need to do—or change—to be the gold standard going forward?

Originally published in December 2004
Reprint R0412C

How Managers' Everyday Decisions Create—or Destroy—Your Company's Strategy

JOSEPH L. BOWER AND CLARK G. GILBERT

Executive Summary

SENIOR EXECUTIVES have long been frustrated by the disconnection between the plans and strategies they devise and the actual behavior of the managers throughout the company. This article approaches the problem from the ground up, recognizing that every time a manager allocates resources, that decision moves the company either into or out of alignment with its announced strategy.

A well-known story—Intel's exit from the memory business—illustrates this point. When discussing what businesses Intel should be in, Andy Grove asked Gordon Moore what they would do if Intel were a company that they had just acquired. When Moore answered, "Get out of memory," they decided to do just that. It turned out, though, that Intel's revenues from memory were by this time only 4% of total sales. Intel's lower-level managers had *already* exited the business. What Intel hadn't done was to shut down the flow of research funding into memory (which was still eating up one-third of all research expenditures); nor had the company announced its exit to the outside world.

Because divisional and operating managers—as well as customers and capital markets—have such a powerful impact on the realized strategy of the firm, senior management might consider focusing less on the company's formal strategy and more on the processes by which the company allocates resources. Top managers must know the track record of the people who are making resource allocation proposals; recognize the strategic issues at stake; reach down to operational managers to work across division lines; frame resource questions to reflect the corporate perspective, especially when large sums of money are involved and conditions are highly uncertain; and create a new context that allows top executives to circumvent the regular resource allocation process when necessary.

OUR FAVORITE STORY about how strategy really gets made comes from a visit one of us—the lead author—made to a large company's headquarters. The company controller was concerned and confused about a capital project proposal he'd recently received from one of the company's most important divisions: a request for a large chimney. Just a chimney. Curious, the controller flew out to visit the division and discovered that division managers had built a whole plant (minus the chimney) using work orders that did not require corporate approval. The chimney was the only portion of the plant that could not be broken down into small enough chunks to escape corporate scrutiny.

The division managers, it seemed, were eager to get on with building a new business and had despaired of getting corporate approval within a reasonable time frame. Convinced that the new capacity was necessary, managers had found a way to build the plant but still needed the chimney. In the end, the division managers were proven right about the need for new capacity and also about the need for speed. The chimney was, ultimately, approved. But who (the controller wondered) was running the company?

We've spent many years, between us, trying to answer that question. In this case, the divisional managers seemed to be calling the shots, at least for their own division. But in general, the answer is more complicated: Senior executives, divisional managers, and operational managers all play a role in deciding which opportunities a company will pursue and which it will pass by (a reasonable definition of "strategy" in the real world). So, for that matter, do customers and the capital markets. What we have found in one research study after another is that how business *really* gets done has little connection to the strategy developed at corporate headquarters. Rather, strategy is crafted, step by step, as managers at all levels of a company—be it a small firm or a large multinational—commit resources to policies, programs, people, and facilities. Because this is true, senior management might consider focusing less attention on thinking through the company's formal strategy and more attention on the processes by which the company allocates resources. Top executives will never be in a position to

call all of the resource-allocation shots—nor should they
be. But they should learn to identify, and influence, the
managers at all levels who can forever alter a company's
future.

How Strategy Gets Made, and Why

A somewhat longer case story will help illuminate the
connection between resource allocation and corporate
strategy. It involves Lou Hughes, who took over as chairman of the executive board of Opel, General Motors'
large European subsidiary, in April 1989. Just seven
months later, in November 1989, the Berlin Wall came
down, and shortly thereafter, Volkswagen, Germany's
number one automobile producer to Opel's number two,
announced a deal with East Germany's state automotive
directorate to lock up all of that country's automotive
manufacturing capacity and to introduce an East
German car in 1994.

A corporate view of strategy making in response to the
tectonic crash of the Berlin Wall would have Hughes's
staff gather information to be relayed to corporate staff,
who would then develop a plan that fit GM's overseas
strategy. (At the time, this strategy was to make cars in
large, modern, focused factories in low-wage countries
such as Spain.) The plan would be debated and then possibly approved by the board of directors. The process
might take a year—especially since very little concrete
data was available on the East German market, and East
Germany was still a sovereign country with its own laws
and currency guarded by 400,000 Soviet soldiers.

Instead, Hughes did as an energetic, entrepreneurial
manager running a large subsidiary in a foreign country
would do: He worked vigorously to secure a place for

Opel in the East German market, in ways that did not fit with corporate strategy and would not have been approved by corporate planners. Rather than waiting to gather data, he created new facts. Acting on an introduction from an Opel union member to the management team of one of the directorate's factories, Hughes negotiated the right to build new capacity in East Germany. He allowed the local factory leader to publicize the deal, induced then-chancellor Helmut Kohl to subsidize the new plant, and drew on talents from other operating divisions of GM to ensure that the facility would be state of the art. GM Europe and corporate headquarters were kept informed, but local decisions drove a steady series of commitments.

As was the case in the chimney story, corporate headquarters was effectively preempted by local management doing what it thought best for the corporation. Despite the apparent contradiction between Opel's plans and corporate strategy, Hughes proposed the commitment of resources, and his proposal was approved first by the European Strategy Board and then by the corporation. Top management (over corporate staff's objections) endorsed Lou Hughes's bottom-up action—and his vision for the future—because he was the local manager, because he had a good track record, and because he was thought to have good judgment. It was more an endorsement of Hughes than of his plan per se.

Does the Opel case demonstrate how resource commitments shape strategy, or is it just an example of an organization out of control? Traditionally minded strategy planners may assume the latter. In fact, the Opel story highlights what we have found to be near universal aspects of the way strategic commitments get made. These fall into two categories.

ORGANIZATIONAL STRUCTURE

The fact that, at any company, responsibility is divided up among various individuals and units has vital consequences for how strategy gets made.

Knowledge is dispersed. For any given strategic question (such as how Opel should enter the East German market), relevant expertise resides in scattered, sometimes unexpected parts of a corporation. When the wall tumbled, managers in the West understood almost nothing about the East German market. The first GM managers to develop any useful knowledge, not surprisingly, were the ones on the spot: Opel's marketing staff. Meanwhile, the GM employees with deep knowledge about lean manufacturing techniques, which would be needed for the new venture, were in California and Canada. Those with the deepest knowledge of overseas strategy and profitability overall were in Detroit, Michigan—but European strategy was developed in Zurich, Switzerland.

Power is dispersed. Lou Hughes's formal authority was limited. He could fund studies and negotiate with East German counterparts, but he could not command his manufacturing director to work with California, nor insist that California work with Opel. The right to approve a plant in a new country lay with the board of GM. For permission to present to the board, Hughes would need to go through GM Europe; in addition, financial and other corporate staff could (and would) provide evaluations of their own. Nonetheless, Hughes's negotiations with the local factory manager and Helmut Kohl could virtually commit GM.

Roles determine perspectives. Miles's Law—the notion that where you stand is a function of where you sit—is central to how strategy gets made in practice. All the managers who would need to cooperate to make an East German initiative possible had different sets of responsibilities for resources and outcomes (like specific levels of sales by model and in total) that shaped their perspectives about what success in a new, eastern European market would look like and what it would be possible to achieve. They all considered a different set of facts, usually those most pertinent to success in their individual operating roles. Hughes's triumph was to convince a group of managers with limited authority that they could deliver on a radical idea.

DECISION-MAKING PROCESSES

Just as important, the way decisions are made throughout an organization has vital consequences for strategy.

Processes span multiple levels; activities proceed on parallel, independent tracks. The notion of a top-down strategic process depends upon central control of all steps in that process. That level of control almost never exists in a large organization—quite the reverse: At the same time that corporate staff is beginning to plan for and roll out initiatives, operating managers invariably are already acting in ways that either undercut or enhance them. Hughes was developing a strong relationship with Helmut Kohl and obtaining funding for a new East German plant even as GM's corporate staff was looking over sales forecasts and planning GM's next moves in Europe: focused factories in countries that probably would not include East Germany.

Processes are iterative. Crafting strategy is an iterative, real-time process; commitments must be made, then either revised or stepped up as new realities emerge. GM's first commitment came when Hughes took part in a factory worker vote that committed the East German spin-out to Opel; this public act made it hard for GM to back out, especially as Hughes was already lobbying with Helmut Kohl for subsidies. A second level of commitment was obtained when GM funded a facility to assemble 10,000 cars, and those cars were presented to German consumers with massive publicity. Soon after, a third stage was reached when a major manufacturing facility was built. GM's strategy for East Germany was revised at each step along the way. How the automaker's European strategy developed after that would turn on events to come, particularly the movement of currencies and labor costs and developments in GM leadership assignments.

Who's in Control?

A leader can announce a strategy to become global, change core technologies, or open new markets, but that strategy will only be realized if it's in line with the pattern of resource allocation decisions made at every level of the organization. Another well-known business story—Intel's exit from the memory business—illustrates this point. Legend has it that Andy Grove and Gordon Moore were talking about what business Intel should be in. Grove asked Moore what they would do if Intel were a company that they had just acquired. When Moore answered, "Get out of memory," Grove suggested that they do just that. It turned out, though, that Intel's revenues from memory were by this time only 4% of its total sales. Intel's lower-level managers had already exited the business. What Intel *hadn't* done was shut down the flow of research funding into memory (which was still eating up one-third of all research expenditures). Nor had the company announced its exit to the outside world.

Because knowledge and power span organizational levels, managers at each level are likely to have an impact on strategy. External forces can also have a strong effect on how resources are allocated, and, in turn, how strategy evolves. The most powerful of these forces are the company's best customers and the capital markets.

GENERAL MANAGERS

Strategic decisions are critically affected not just by senior corporate managers, but also by midlevel general managers, their teams, and the operating managers who report to them. These intermediate-level general managers run the fundamental processes that make multi-business, multinational companies feasible. They are general managers who report to other general managers. Their jobs involve translating broad corporate objectives such as earnings and growth into specifics that operating managers can understand and execute on. They provide corporate management with an integrated picture of what their businesses can accomplish today and might achieve in the future by determining the package of plans, programs, and activities that should drive the strategy for that business.

One of the most obvious ways that these managers in the middle affect strategy is through their decisions about which proposals to send upward for corporate review. One top executive we interviewed communicated his surprised realization of this role: "One fascinating moment came as I met with a key midlevel manager. I had mapped out on a piece of paper the resource allocation process and its effect on the intended and emergent strategies. As we talked, this manager proudly told me that he was the one who set the strategy, not the CEO or board of directors. According to him, he owned the resource allocation process because his boss, who was president of the largest business unit, would not approve anything without his recommendation."

OPERATIONAL MANAGERS

Most strategy analysts ignore the role operating managers have on strategy outcomes, assuming that these managers are too tied to the operational requirements of the business to think strategically. Senior executives overlook the very real impact of operating managers at their peril. For example, in 2000, Toyota launched the Echo, a no-frills vehicle designed partly to protect Toyota from low-cost competition. But deep inside that organization sat salespeople in local retail operations. Because margins (and, more important, sales commissions) were higher on other Toyota vehicles, customers were repeatedly steered toward higher-priced models. Even though the corporate office placed a high priority on the new product, the day-to-day operating decisions of the organization directed the realized strategy of the firm elsewhere.

From the Toyota example, one might conclude that operating managers (salespeople, in this case) constrain innovation because they are not aligned with the strategy of the firm. However, operating managers can redirect and improve strategy in very innovative ways. At Intel, the exit from memory took place over time, because the managers in manufacturing responded to a

directive from finance: Allocate plant space so as to maximize gross margin per wafer square inch. Memory and
microprocessors used the same silicon wafers, so as competitive conditions worsened in memory, the rule took
Intel right out of the business.

CUSTOMERS

Customer decisions can play a huge role in real strategy
formation, particularly in businesses with a few very
powerful customers. Companies that stay close to their
best customers give them a virtual veto on product
development and distribution. By the mid-1990s, Tony
Ridder at Knight Ridder recognized that the Internet was
going to have a dramatic effect on his newspaper company. Accordingly, he redirected corporate strategy to
focus on the Internet, presented annual reports that discussed plans for new media, and moved the headquarters from Miami to San Jose. Despite these bold efforts to
change the corporate strategy, the realized strategy continued to be largely controlled by existing advertising
customers in the newspaper business. Every day, sales
reps had the choice of selling a $40,000 print display ad
to their existing print customers or promoting a $2,000
online ad that was unfamiliar, even uninteresting, to
these same advertisers. And every day, the sales reps
made the logical choice to sell traditional print ads.
Despite the explosive growth in online advertising,
Knight Ridder and other newspaper companies were
largely unsuccessful at tapping into this new and evolving revenue stream. Through their influence on the sales
force, the print advertising customers effectively captured the newspapers' resource allocation process and, in
effect, its strategy.

CAPITAL MARKETS

Most observers understand that capital markets influence management performance. That they can dramatically reshape strategy is less well documented, but equally true. Earnings pressure can cause a company to exit a market too soon; a dip in stock price can cause a company to scramble to improve short-term performance. One of the clearest cases of this phenomenon comes from a natural experiment in the U.S. telephony market that one of our doctoral students examined. BellSouth and U.S. West were two Baby Bells that formed when AT&T was broken up. Both were born with the same technology, patents, and planning models. Despite their similarities, the capital markets determined that U.S. West's growth prospects were inferior to those of its sibling. In the face of the consequent pressure on earnings, U.S. West's CEO chose to diversify by moving away from regulated telephony and to set high earnings objectives. To meet those objectives, the managers of the cellular business (the general managers in the middle) adopted a strategy of skimming, that is, seeking high margins on the low-volume top end of the market.

Facing less-intense short-term pressure from the capital markets, BellSouth chose to treat cellular as an opportunity with earning potential equal to that of its wire line business and with much better growth prospects. Managers pursued a strategy of broad market penetration.

BellSouth's and U.S. West's strategic objectives were reflected in the performance measures that were set for the two businesses. Despite similar early performance, the different measures led the two companies to reach very different conclusions about the cellular market. U.S.

West was disappointed by results that failed to reach the high financial targets it had set. BellSouth was pleased with the positive first steps and made further investments. U.S. West ultimately divested its business, while BellSouth became one of the leading cellular providers.

Manage It Anyway!

If divisional, middle, and operating managers—as well as customers and capital markets—have such a powerful impact on the resource allocation process and, in turn, on the realized strategy of the firm, what does that imply for the role of corporate leaders? Is the process of strategy formation entirely out of their hands? Of course not. We believe that the complexity of the resource allocation process only increases the need for leadership at the top. But senior leaders have to understand what is happening and adjust their management styles accordingly. Here are six ways that senior managers can direct the strategy of their firm by better understanding the resource allocation process.

Understand the people whose names are on the proposals you read. When you read a proposal to commit scarce people or capital, you should calibrate what you are reading against the track record of the executive who signed the document. If the signing executive has a near-perfect record of proposals implemented, then you know that there is probably little downside in what you are reading, but the upside may be significantly underexploited. Requests for resources are based on stories about the future. Those stories may be summarized with numbers, but they represent judgments about uncertain developments. Very often, your managers' judgment—and your capacity to judge their judgment!—is more important than the actual numbers presented. This reality will kill your finance staff, because they are good at crunching numbers, not at gauging what managers understand and what they don't.

Recognize the strategic issue, and make sure it is addressed. Almost always, requests for resources require making two decisions: *Should we support this business idea?* and *Is this proposal the right way to go about it?* Most capital budgeting processes are set up to vet projects (in other words, they're aimed at the second question, not the first). It is usually possible to carry out fairly rigorous quantitative analysis comparing the plan of action in a proposal with alternatives. It is important that this analysis be done—and it is often done ad nauseam. But our research shows that the first question, the *business* question, is more important and far more difficult to answer—and it is often ignored. It is easy to invest money in cost-saving projects that will earn precisely the returns forecast in businesses that are losing money overall. After the project, they just lose less. One of our studies showed that companies and their industries poured new money into old technology at the same time that they were investing in facilities based on new technology that made the first set of investments obsolete. Managing resource allocation to build sound strategy requires that the proposal evaluation process begin with the "should we" question. Should we put a plant in East Germany? In the end, you may decide to back managers rather than their logic, because you want to support them. But do it with your eyes open and controls in place.

When a debate reflects fundamental differences about the strategy, intervene. The "should we" question inevitably focuses on basic issues about how the company wants to compete. It almost always involves evaluating different views that reflect the positions of the executives in question. Lou Hughes thought that he could use a new East German facility to drive change at Opel's main plant. Some at GM headquarters thought it more important to continue expansion at low-cost sites in southern Europe and Latin America. Smart executives use resource allocation opportunities like a new Opel plant in East Germany to trigger strategic discussions that cross organizational perspectives. They bring together managers with different kinds of knowledge to discuss the evolution of strategy, not the details of a project proposal. Andy Grove calls this "getting knowledge power and position power in the same room at the same time." Top executives will almost always have to convene that meeting and pay attention to who is invited. They will also have to work hard to create a collaborative environment.

Use operational managers to get work done across divisional lines. When top managers believe that the right way to serve a market will require two or more divisions to cooperate, they face an immediate problem. Divisional managers obsess about the prospects for their own businesses. A bottom-up approach does not naturally foster cooperation because these managers view the resource allocation process as a way to protect their turf. (They also come at the same strategy question from quite different perspectives—Miles's Law!) Because of this, executives need to reach down to operational managers if they want divisions to cooperate. If freed from divisional measurement and compensation systems, operating talent can be engaged by the opportunity to serve customers better. It won't happen automatically, but we have seen numerous cases in which cross-divisional teams that were assembled and supported by top leadership have been able to work together, even when their divisional superiors resisted the project. For example, marketing services giant WPP successfully created virtual companies, made up of staff from various units, to focus on retail and health care markets. While some division heads saw this as an encroachment on their mandate in these areas, the operating managers reveled in their ability to collectively solve client problems. Of course, the easiest way for a division head to undermine such a project is to deny it the right people. Top managers must make sure that the right questions are asked and that the right people are made available to work on those questions.

The leadership has to connect the dots. Understand that bottom-up resource allocation processes do not add up to a corporate view. Top management may have to lay out the big picture when more than one division is (or ought to be) involved in a strategy question. When bottom-up processes are at work, several problems can occur. Conflicting divisional perspectives tend to resolve themselves on the basis of which unit has the most power. Or, divisional managers make compromises that share resources in ways that seem fair on paper but are not the best approach strategically. Worse, a division may agree—explicitly or tacitly—not to challenge another division's proposals in return for the same treatment. In many companies, that is the norm. It will be

sheer coincidence if the result of this system is what the
company could achieve if the divisions were working
together with a coherent plan. Top management needs
to step in and frame questions that reflect the corporate
perspective, especially when large sums of money are
involved and conditions are highly uncertain. They must
get divisions to ask, "What's best for the company?"

**Create a new context that allows leadership to
circumvent the regular resource allocation
process.** Most out-of-the-box or disruptive ideas are
badly handled by a bottom-up resource allocation process. It is top management that has to ask, "Is there a
technology under development that looks inferior or
uncertain today but will undermine our business from
beneath once it is properly developed?" Windows NT
had this impact on UNIX applications, for example, as
did Internet applications on a host of industries. It takes
a very well-informed paranoia to ask this question early
enough to keep a strong company in the lead. A decision
to pursue out-of-the-box ideas often requires a new box:
a separate organizational unit with a new location,
milestone-type measures instead of annual budgets, and
short reporting lines to the top.

THE IMPLICATION of these six recommendations is
really a meta-recommendation. Once you realize that
resource allocation decisions make your strategy, then
you know you can't rely on a system to manage the
resource allocation process. No planning or capital-
budgeting procedure can substitute for the best leaders
in the company making considered judgments about
how to allocate resources. No system of incentives will

align divisional objectives so that new opportunities will be studied with the corporate interest in mind. Because of its impact on strategy, the corporate senior management has to engage itself—selectively, to be sure—in the debates that mark inflection points in the process.

This is where top-down process is vital. If you're part of the leadership, you can't delegate responsibility for your company's direction. At Intel and Opel, divisional managers took the right action. But that is often not the case. The management of the mining or semiconductor divisions at GE didn't tell Jack Welch to divest. The management of the television set businesses did not tell Frank Dangeard to shift Thomson into digital post-production. Quite the contrary, those divisional managers were generating proposals to grow their businesses. The leadership challenge is to give coherent direction to how resources are allocated and, by doing so, align the bottom-up processes with top-down objectives. That's how you drive strategy in a big organization.

Originally published in February 2007
Reprint R0702C

Stop Making Plans; Start Making Decisions

MICHAEL C. MANKINS AND

RICHARD STEELE

Executive Summary

MANY EXECUTIVES have grown skeptical of strategic planning. Is it any wonder? Despite all the time and energy that go into it, strategic planning most often acts as a barrier to good decision making and does little to influence strategy.

Strategic planning fails because of two factors: It typically occurs annually, and it focuses on individual business units. As such, the process is completely at odds with the way executives actually make important strategy decisions, which are neither constrained by the calendar nor defined by unit boundaries. Thus, according to a survey of 156 large companies, senior executives often make strategic decisions outside the planning process, in an ad hoc fashion and without rigorous analysis or productive debate.

But companies can fix the process if they attack its root problems. A few forward-looking firms have thrown out their calendar-driven, business-unit-focused planning procedures and replaced them with continuous, issues-focused decision making. In doing so, they rely on several basic principles: They separate, but integrate, decision making and plan making. They focus on a few key themes. And they structure strategy reviews to produce real decisions.

When companies change the timing and focus of strategic planning, they also change the nature of senior management's discussions about strategy—from "review and approve" to "debate and decide," in which top executives actively think through every major decision and its implications for the company's performance and value. The authors have found that these companies make more than twice as many important strategic decisions per year as companies that follow the traditional planning model.

Is STRATEGIC PLANNING completely useless? That was the question the CEO of a global manufacturer recently asked himself. Two years earlier, he had launched an ambitious overhaul of the company's planning process. The old approach, which required business-unit heads to make regular presentations to the firm's executive committee, had broken down entirely. The ExCom members—the CEO, COO, CFO, CTO, and head of HR— had grown tired of sitting through endless PowerPoint presentations that provided them few opportunities to challenge the business units' assumptions or influence their strategies. And the unit heads had complained that the ExCom reviews were long on exhortation but short on executable advice. Worse, the reviews led to very few worthwhile decisions.

The revamped process incorporated state-of-the-art thinking about strategic planning. To avoid information overload, it limited each business to 15 "high-impact" exhibits describing the unit's strategy. To ensure thoughtful discussions, it required that all presentations and supporting materials be distributed to the ExCom at least a week in advance. The review sessions themselves were restructured to allow ample time for give-and-take between the corporate team and the business-unit executives. And rather than force the unit heads to traipse off to headquarters for meetings, the ExCom agreed to spend an unprecedented six weeks each spring visiting all 22 units for daylong sessions. The intent was to make the strategy reviews longer, more focused, and more consequential.

It didn't work. After using the new process for two planning cycles, the CEO gathered feedback from the participants through an anonymous survey. To his dismay, the report contained a litany of complaints: "It takes too much time." "It's at too high a level." "It's disconnected from the way we run the business." And so on. Most damning of all, however, was the respondents' near-universal view that the new approach produced very few real decisions. The CEO was dumbfounded. How could the company's cutting-edge planning process still be so badly broken? More important, what should he do to make strategic planning drive more, better, and faster decisions?

Like this CEO, many executives have grown skeptical of strategic planning. Is it any wonder? Despite all the time and energy most companies put into strategic planning, the process is most often a barrier to good decision making, our research indicates. As a result, strategic planning doesn't really influence most companies' strategy.

In the following pages, we will demonstrate that the failure of most strategic planning is due to two factors: It is typically an annual process, and it is most often focused on individual business units. As such, the process is completely at odds with the way executives actually make important strategy decisions, which are neither constrained by the calendar nor defined by unit boundaries. Not surprisingly, then, senior executives routinely sidestep the planning process. They make the decisions that really shape their company's strategy and determine its future—decisions about mergers and acquisitions, product launches, corporate restructurings, and the like—outside the planning process, typically in an ad hoc fashion, without rigorous analysis or productive debate. Critical decisions are made incorrectly or not at all. More than anything else, this disconnect— between the way planning works and the way decision making happens—explains the frustration, if not outright antipathy, most executives feel toward strategic planning. (See the sidebar "The Disconnect Between Planning and Decision Making" at the end of this article.)

But companies can fix the process if they attack its root problems. A small number of forward-looking companies have thrown out their calendar-driven, business-unit-focused planning processes and replaced them with continuous, issues-focused decision making. By changing the timing and focus of strategic planning, they've also changed the nature of top management's discussions about strategy—from "review and approve" to "debate and decide," meaning that senior executives seriously think through every major decision and its implications for the company's performance and value. Indeed, these companies use the strategy development process to drive decision making. As a consequence, they make more than twice as many important strategic decisions each year as companies that follow the traditional planning model. (See "Who Makes More Decisions?" at the end of this article.) These companies have stopped making plans and started making decisions.

Where Planning Goes Wrong

In the fall of 2005, Marakon Associates, in collaboration with the Economist Intelligence Unit, surveyed senior executives from 156 large companies worldwide, all with sales of $1 billion or more (40% of them had revenues over $10 billion). We asked these executives how their companies developed long-range plans and how effectively they thought their planning processes drove strategic decisions.

The results of the survey confirmed what we have observed over many years of consulting: The timing and structure of strategic planning are obstacles to good decision making. Specifically, we found that companies with standard planning processes and practices make only 2.5 major strategic decisions each year, on average (by "major," we mean they have the potential to increase company profits by 10% or more over the long term). It's hard to imagine that with so few strategic decisions driving growth, these companies can keep moving forward and deliver the financial performance that investors expect.

Even worse, we suspect that the few decisions companies do reach are made in spite of the strategic planning process, not because of it. Indeed, the traditional planning model is so cumbersome and out of sync with the way executives want and need to make decisions that top managers all too often sidestep the process when making their biggest strategic choices.

With the big decisions being made outside the planning process, strategic planning becomes merely a codification of judgments top management has already made, rather than a vehicle for identifying and debating the critical decisions that the company needs to make to produce superior performance. Over time, managers begin to question the value of strategic planning, withdraw from it, and come to rely on other processes for setting company strategy.

THE CALENDAR EFFECT

At 66% of the companies in our survey, planning is a periodic event, often conducted as a precursor to the yearly budgeting and capital-approval processes. In fact, linking strategic planning to these other management processes is often cited as a best practice. But forcing strategic planning into an annual cycle risks making it irrelevant to executives, who must make many important decisions throughout the year.

There are two major drawbacks to such a rigid schedule. The first might be called the *time* problem. A once-a-year planning schedule simply does not give executives sufficient time to address the issues that most affect performance. According to our survey, companies that follow an annual planning calendar devote less than nine weeks per year to strategy development. That's barely two months to collect relevant facts, set strategic priorities, weigh competing alternatives, and make important strategic choices. Many issues—particularly those spanning multiple businesses, crossing geographic boundaries, or involving entire value chains—cannot be resolved effectively in such a short time. It took Boeing, for example, almost two years to decide to outsource major activities such as wing manufacturing.

Constrained by the planning calendar, corporate executives face two choices: They can either not address these complex issues—in effect, throwing them in the "too-hard" bucket—or they can address them through some process other than strategic planning. In both cases, strategic planning is marginalized and separated from strategic decision making.

Then there's the *timing* problem. Even when executives allot sufficient time in strategy development to address tough issues, the timing of the process can create problems. At most companies, strategic planning is a batch process in which managers analyze market and competitor information, identify threats and opportunities, and then define a multiyear plan. But in the real world, managers make strategic decisions continuously, often motivated by an immediate need for action (or reaction). When a new competitor enters a market, for instance, or a rival introduces a new technology, executives must act quickly and decisively to safeguard the company's performance. But very few companies (less than 10%, according to our survey) have any sort of rigorous or disciplined process for responding to changes in the external environment. Instead, managers rely on ad hoc processes to correct course or make opportunistic moves. Once again, strategic planning is sidelined, and executives risk making poor decisions that have not been carefully thought through.

M&A decisions provide a particularly egregious example of the timing problem. Acquisition opportunities tend to emerge spontaneously, the result of changes in management at a target company, the actions of a competitor, or some other unpredictable event. Faced with a promising opportunity and limited time in which to act, executives can't wait until the opportunity is evaluated as part of the next annual planning cycle, so they assess the deal and make a quick decision. But because there's often no proper review process, the softer customer- and people-related issues so critical to effective integration of an acquired company can get short-changed. It is no coincidence that failure to plan for integration is often cited as the primary cause of deal failure.

THE BUSINESS-UNIT EFFECT

The organizational focus of the typical planning process compounds its calendar effects—or, perhaps more aptly, defects. Two-thirds of the executives we surveyed indicated that strategic planning at their companies is conducted business by business—that is, it is focused on units or groups of units. But 70% of the senior executives who responded to our survey stated they make decisions issue by issue. For example, should we enter China? Should we outsource manufacturing? Should we acquire our distributor? Given this mismatch between the way planning is organized and the way big decisions are made, it's hardly surprising that, once again, corporate leaders look elsewhere for guidance and inspiration. In fact, only 11% of the executives we surveyed believed strongly that planning was worth the effort.

The organizational focus of traditional strategic planning also creates distance, even antagonism, between corporate executives and business-unit managers. Consider, for example, the way most companies conduct strategy reviews—as formal meetings between senior managers and the heads of each business unit. While these reviews are intended to produce a fact-based dialogue, they often amount to little more than business tourism. The executive committee flies in for a day, sees the sights, meets the natives, and flies out. The business unit, for its part, puts in a lot of work preparing for this royal visit and is keen to make it smooth and trouble free. The unit hopes to escape with few unanswered questions and an approved plan. Accordingly, local managers control the flow of information upward, and senior managers are presented only with information that shows each unit in the best possible light. Opportunities are highlighted; threats are downplayed or omitted.

Even if there's no subterfuge, senior corporate managers still have trouble engaging in constructive dialogue and debate because of what might be called information asymmetry. They just don't have the information they need to be helpful in guiding business units. So when they're presented with a strategic plan that's too good to be believed, they have only two real options: either reject it—a move that's all but unheard-of at most large companies—or play along and impose stretch targets to secure at least the promise that the unit will improve performance. In both cases, the review does little to drive decisions on issues. It's hardly surprising that only 13% of the executives we surveyed felt that top managers were effectively engaged in all aspects of strategy development at their companies—from target setting to debating alternatives to approving strategies and allocating resources.

Decision-Focused Strategic Planning

Strategic planning can't have impact if it doesn't drive decision making. And it can't drive decision making as long as it remains focused on individual business units and limited by the calendar. Over the past several years, we have observed that many of the best-performing companies have abandoned the traditional approach and are focusing explicitly on reaching decisions through the continuous identification and systematic resolution of strategic issues. (The "Continuous, Decision-Oriented Planning" at the end of this article presents a detailed example of the issues-oriented approach.) Although these companies have found different specific solutions, all have made essentially the same fundamental changes to their planning and strategy development processes in order to produce more, better, and faster decisions.

They separate—but integrate—decision making and plan making. First and most important, a company must take decisions out of the traditional planning process and create a different, parallel process for developing strategy that helps executives identify the decisions they *need to make* to create more shareholder value over time. The output of this new process isn't a plan at all—it's a set of concrete decisions that management can codify into future business plans through the existing planning process, which remains in place. Identifying and making decisions is distinct from creating, monitoring, and updating a strategic plan, and the two sets of tasks require very different, but integrated, processes.

Boeing Commercial Airplanes (BCA) is a case in point. This business unit, Boeing's largest, has had a long-range business plan (LRBP) process for many years. The protracted cycles of commercial aircraft production require the unit's CEO, Alan Mulally, and his leadership team to take a long-term view of the business. Accordingly, the unit's LRBP contains a ten-year financial forecast, including projected revenues, backlogs, operating margins, and capital investments. BCA's leadership team reviews the business plan weekly to track the division's performance relative to the plan and to keep the organization focused on execution.

The weekly reviews were invaluable as a performance-monitoring tool at BCA, but they were not particularly effective at bringing new issues to the surface or driving strategic decision making. So in 2001, the unit's leadership team introduced a Strategy Integration Process focused on uncovering and addressing the business's most important strategic issues (such as determining the best go-to-market strategy for the business, driving the evolution of BCA's product strategy, or fueling growth in services). The team assigned to this process holds strategy integration meetings every Monday to track BCA's progress in resolving these long-term issues. Once a specific course of action is agreed upon and approved by BCA's leadership team, the long-range business plan is updated at the next weekly review to reflect the projected change in financial performance.

The time invested in the new decision-making process is more than compensated for by the time saved in the LRBP process, which is now solely focused on strategy execution. The company gets the best of both worlds—disciplined decision making and superior execution. BCA has maintained the value of the LRBP as an execution tool even as it has increased the quality and quantity of important decisions. Managers believe that the new process is at least partially responsible for the sharp turnaround in Boeing's performance since 2001.

They focus on a few key themes. High-performing companies typically focus their strategy discussions on a limited number of important issues or themes, many of which span multiple businesses. Moving away from a business-by-business planning model in this way has proved particularly helpful for large, complex organizations, where strategy discussions can quickly get bogged down as each division manager attempts to cover every aspect of the unit's strategy. Business-unit managers should remain involved in corporate-level strategy planning that affects their units. But a focus on issues rather than business units better aligns strategy development with decision making and investment.

Consider Microsoft. The world's leading software maker is a highly matrixed organization. No strategy can be effectively executed at the company without careful coordination across multiple functions and across two or more of Microsoft's seven business units, or, as executives refer to them, "P&Ls"—Client; Server and Tools; Information Worker; MSN; Microsoft Business Solutions; Mobile and Embedded Devices; and Home and Entertainment. In late 2004, faced with a perceived shortage of good investment ideas, CEO Steve Ballmer asked Robert Uhlaner, Microsoft's corporate vice president of strategy, planning, and analysis, to devise a new strategic planning process for the company. Uhlaner put in place a Growth and Performance Planning Process that starts with agreement by Ballmer's leadership team on a set of strategic themes—major issues like PC market growth, the entertainment market, and security—that cross business-unit boundaries. These themes not only frame the dialogue for Microsoft's annual strategy review, they also guide the units in fleshing out investment alternatives to fuel the company's growth. Dialogues between the P&L leaders and Ballmer's team focus on what the company can do to address each strategic theme, rather than on individual unit strategies. The early results of

this new process are promising. "You have to be careful
what you wish for," Uhlaner says. "Our new process has
surfaced countless new opportunities for growth. We no
longer worry about a dearth of investment ideas, but
how best to fund them."

Like Microsoft, Diageo North America—a division of
the international beer, wine, and spirits marketer—has
recently changed the way it conducts strategic planning
to allocate resources across its diverse portfolio. Diageo
historically focused its planning efforts on individual
brands. Brand managers were allowed to make the case
for additional investment, no matter what the size of the
brand or its strategic role in the portfolio. As a result,
resource allocation was bedeviled by endless negotiations between the brands and corporate management.
This political wrangling made it extremely difficult for
Diageo's senior managers to establish a consistent
approach to growth, because a lack of transparency pre-
vented them from discerning, from the many requests
for additional funding, which brands really deserved
more resources and which did not.

Starting in 2001, Diageo overhauled its approach to
strategy development. A crucial change was to focus
planning on the factors that the company believed would
most drive market growth—for example, an increase in
the U.S. Hispanic population. By modeling the impact of
these factors on the brand portfolio, Diageo has been
better able to match its resources with the brands that
have the most growth potential so that it can specify
the strategies and investments each brand manager
should develop, says Jim Moseley, senior vice president
of consumer planning and research for Diageo North
America. For example, the division now identifies certain
brands for growth and earmarks specific resources for

investment in these units. This focused approach has enabled the company to shorten the brand planning process and reduce the time spent on negotiations between the brands and division management. It has also given senior management greater confidence in each brand's ability to contribute to Diageo's growth.

They make strategy development continuous. Effective strategy planners spread strategy reviews throughout the year rather than squeeze them into a two- or three-month window. This allows senior executives to focus on one issue at a time until they reach a decision or set of decisions. Moreover, managers can add issues to the agenda as market and competitive conditions change, so there's no need for ad hoc processes. Senior executives can thus rely on a single strategic planning process—or, perhaps more aptly, a single strategic decision-making model—to drive decision making across the company.

Textron, a $10 billion multi-industry company, has implemented a new, continuous strategy-development process built around a prioritized "decision agenda" comprising the company's most important issues and opportunities. Until 2004, Textron had a fairly traditional strategic planning process. Each spring, the company's operating units—businesses as diverse as Bell Helicopter, E-Z-Go golf cars, and Jacobsen turf maintenance equipment—would develop a five-year strategic plan based on standard templates. Unit managers would then review their strategic plans with Textron's management committee (the company's top five executives) during day-long sessions at each unit. Once the strategy reviews were complete, the units incorporated the results, as best they could, into their annual operating plans and capital budgets.

In June 2004, dissatisfied with the quality and pace of the decision making that resulted from the company's strategy reviews, CEO Lewis Campbell asked Stuart Grief, Textron's vice president for strategy and business development, to rethink the company's strategic planning process. After carefully reviewing the company's practices and gathering feedback from its 30 top executives, Grief and his team designed a new Textron Strategy Process.

There were two important changes. First, rather than concentrate all of the operating-unit strategy reviews in the second quarter of each year, the company now spreads strategy dialogues throughout the year—two to three units are reviewed per quarter. Second, rather than organize the management committee dialogues around business-unit plans, Textron now holds continuous reviews that are designed to address each strategic issue on the company's decision agenda. Both changes have enabled Textron's management committee to be much more effectively engaged in business-unit strategy development. The changes have also ensured that there's a forum in which cross-unit issues can be raised and addressed by top management, with input from relevant business-unit managers. The process has significantly increased the number of strategic decisions the company makes each year. As a result, Textron has gone from being an also-ran among its multi-industrial peers to a top-quartile performer over the past 18 months.

John Cullivan, the director of strategy at Cardinal Health, one of the world's leading healthcare products and services companies, reports similar benefits from shifting to a continuous planning model. "Continuous decision making is tough to establish because it requires the reallocation of management time at the top levels of the company," he says. "But the process has enabled us to get sharper focus on the short-term performance of our vertical businesses and make faster progress on our longer-term priorities, some of which are horizontal opportunities that cut across businesses and thus are difficult to manage."

To facilitate continuous strategic decision making, Cardinal has made a series of important changes to its traditional planning process. At the corporate level, for example, the company has put in place a rolling six-month agenda for its executive committee dialogues, a practice that allows everyone inside Cardinal to know what issues management is working on and when decisions will be reached. Similar decision agendas are used at the business-unit and functional levels, ensuring that common standards are applied to all important decisions at the company. And to support continuous decision making at Cardinal, the company has trained "black belts" in new analytical tools and processes and deployed them throughout the organization. This provides each of the company's businesses and functions with the resources needed to address strategic priorities that emerge over time.

They structure strategy reviews to produce real decisions.   The most common obstacles to decision making at large companies are disagreements among executives over past decisions, current alternatives, and even the facts presented to support strategic plans. Leading companies structure their strategy review sessions to overcome these problems.

At Textron, for example, strategic-issue reviews are organized around "facts, alternatives, and choices." Each issue is addressed in two half-day sessions with the company's management committee, allowing for eight to ten issues to be resolved throughout the year. In the first session, the management committee debates and reaches agreement on the relevant facts—information on the profitability of key markets, the actions of competitors, the purchase behavior of customers, and so on—and a limited set of viable strategy alternatives. The purpose of this first meeting is not to reach agreement on a specific course of action; rather, the meeting ensures that the group has the best possible information and a robust set of alternatives to consider. The second session is focused on evaluating these alternatives from a strategic and financial perspective and selecting the best course of action. By separating the dialogue around facts and alternatives from the debate over choices, Textron's management committee avoids many of the bottlenecks that plague strategic decision making at most companies and reaches many more decisions than it otherwise would.

Like Textron, Cadbury Schweppes has changed the structure of its strategy dialogues to focus top managers more explicitly on decision making. In 2002, after acquiring and integrating gum-maker Adams—a move that significantly expanded Cadbury's product and geographic reach—the company realized it needed to rethink how it was conducting dialogues about strategy between the corporate center and the businesses. The company made two important changes. First, strategy dialogues were redesigned to incorporate a standard set of facts and metrics about consumers, customers, and competitors. This information helped get critical commercial choices in front of top managers, so that the choices were no longer buried in the business units. Second, senior executives' time was reallocated so they could pay more attention to markets that were crucial to realizing Cadbury's ten-year vision and to making important decisions.

Cadbury's top team now spends one full week per year in each of the countries that are most critical to driving the company's performance, so that important decisions can be informed by direct observation as well as through indirect analysis. Strategy dialogues are now based on a much deeper understanding of the markets. Cadbury's strategic reviews no longer merely consist of reviews of and approval of a strategic plan, and they produce many more important decisions.

D ONE RIGHT, strategic planning can have an enormous impact on a company's performance and long-term value. By creating a planning process that enables managers to discover great numbers of hidden strategic issues and make more decisions, companies will open the door to many more opportunities for long-term growth and profitability. By embracing decision-focused planning, companies will almost certainly find that the quantity and quality of their decisions will improve. And—no coincidence—they will discover an improvement in the quality of the dialogue between senior corporate managers and unit managers. Corporate executives will gain a better understanding of the challenges their companies face, and unit managers will benefit fully from the experience and insights of the company's leaders. As Mark Reckitt, a director of group strategy at Cadbury Schweppes, puts it: "Continuous, decision-focused strategic planning has helped our top management team to streamline its agenda and work with business units and functional management to make far better business-strategy and commercial decisions."

Who Makes More Decisions?

COMPANIES SEE a dramatic increase in the quality of their decision making once they abandon the traditional planning model, which is calendar driven and focused on the business units. In our survey, the companies that broke most completely with the past made more than twice as many strategic decisions each year as companies wedded to tradition. What's more, the new structure of the planning process ensures that the decisions are probably the best that could have been made, given the information available to managers at the time.

Here are the average numbers of major strategic decisions reached per year in companies that take the following approaches to strategic planning:

Annual review focused on business units
2.5 decisions per year

Annual review focused on issues
3.5 decisions per year

Continuous review focused on business units
4.1 decisions per year

Continuous review focused on issues
6.1 decisions per year

Source: Marakon Associates and the Economist Intelligence Unit

Traditional Planning

COMPANIES THAT FOLLOW the traditional strategic planning model develop a strategy plan for each business unit at some point during the year. A cross-functional team dedicates less than nine weeks to developing the unit's plan. The executive committee reviews each plan—typically in daylong, on-site meetings—and rubber-stamps the results. The plans are consolidated to produce a companywide strategic plan for review by the board of directors.

Once the strategic-planning cycle is complete, the units dedicate another eight to nine weeks to budgeting and capital planning (in most companies, these processes are not explicitly linked to strategic planning).

The executive committee then holds another round of meetings with each of the business units to negotiate performance targets, resource commitments, and (in many cases) compensation for managers.

The results: an approved but potentially unrealistic strategic plan for each business unit and a separate budget for each unit that is decoupled from the unit's strategic plan.

Continuous, Decision-Oriented Planning

ONCE THE COMPANY as a whole has identified its most important strategic priorities (typically in an annual strategy update), executive committee dialogues, spread throughout the year, are set up to reach decisions on as many issues as possible. Since issues frequently span multiple business units, task forces are established to prepare the strategic and financial information that's needed to uncover and evaluate strategy alternatives for each issue. Preparation time may exceed nine weeks. The executive committee engages in two dialogues for each issue at three to four hours each. The first dialogue

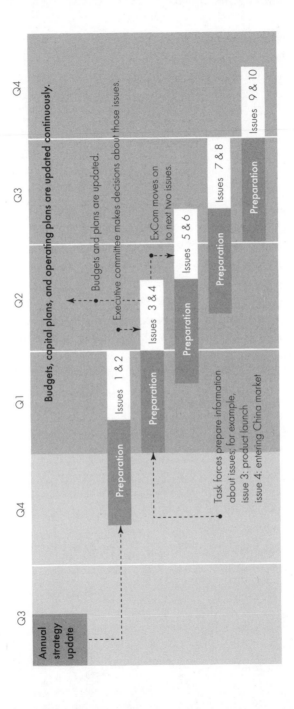

Q3 | Q4 | Q1 | Q2 | Q3 | Q4

Annual strategy update

Preparation — Issues 1 & 2

Preparation — Issues 3 & 4

Preparation — Issues 5 & 6

Preparation — Issues 7 & 8

Preparation — Issues 9 & 10

Budgets, capital plans, and operating plans are updated continuously.

Budgets and plans are updated.

Executive committee makes decisions about those issues.

ExCom moves on to next two issues.

Task forces prepare information about issues; for example, issue 3: product launch issue 4: entering China market focuses on reaching agreement on the facts surrounding the issue and on a set of viable alternatives. The second focuses on the evaluation of those alternatives and the selection of the best course of action. Once an issue is resolved, a new one is added to the agenda. Critical issues can be inserted into the planning process at any time as market and competitive conditions change.

Once a decision has been reached, the budgets and capital plans for the affected business units are updated to reflect the selected option. Consequently, the strategic-planning process and the capital and budgeting processes are integrated. This significantly reduces the need for lengthy negotiations between the executive committee and unit management over the budget and capital plan.

The results: a concrete plan for addressing each key issue; for each business unit, a continuously updated budget and capital plan that is linked directly to the resolution of critical strategic issues; and more, faster, better decisions per year.

The Disconnect Between Planning and Decision Making

How Executives Plan

66% periodically

Percentage of surveyed executives saying their companies conduct strategic planning only at prescribed times

How Executives Decide

100% continuously

Percentage of executives saying strategic decisions are made without regard to the calendar

67% unit by unit

Percentage saying planning is done unit by unit

70% issue by issue

Percentage saying decisions are made issue by issue

No wonder only **11%** of executives are highly satisfied that strategic planning is worth the effort.

Originally published in January 2006
Reprint R0601F

The Tools of Cooperation and Change

CLAYTON M. CHRISTENSEN, MATT MARX,

AND HOWARD H. STEVENSON

Executive Summary

EMPLOYERS CAN CHOOSE from lots of tools when they want to encourage employees to work together toward a new corporate goal. One of the rarest managerial skills is the ability to understand which tools will work in a given situation and which will misfire.

Cooperation tools fall into four major categories: power, management, leadership, and culture. Choosing the right tool, say the authors, requires assessing the organization along two critical dimensions: the extent to which people agree on *what they want* and the extent to which they agree on *cause and effect,* or how to get what they want. The authors plot on a matrix where various organizations fall along these two dimensions. Employees represented in the lower-left quadrant of the model, for example, disagree strongly both about what they want and on what actions will produce which results. Those in the upper-right quadrant agree on both dimensions.

Different quadrants call for different tools. When employees share little consensus on either dimension, for instance, the only methods that will elicit cooperation are "power tools" such as fiat, force, and threats. Yugoslavia's Josip Broz Tito wielded such devices effectively. So did Jamie Dimon, current CEO of JPMorgan Chase, during the bank's integration with Bank One. For employees who agree on what they want but not on how to get it—think of Microsoft in 1995—leadership tools, such as vision statements, are more appropriate.

Some leaders are blessed with an instinct for choosing the right tools—Continental Airlines' Gordon Bethune, General Electric's Jack Welch, and IBM's Lou Gerstner are all examples. Others can use this framework to help select the most appropriate tools for their circumstances.

THE PRIMARY TASK of management is to get people to work together in a systematic way. Like orchestra conductors, managers direct the talents and actions of various players to produce a desired result. It's a complicated job, and it becomes much more so when managers are trying to get people to change, rather than continue with the status quo. Even the best CEOs can stumble in their attempts to encourage people to work together toward a new corporate goal.

In 1999, for example, Procter & Gamble's Durk Jager, a highly regarded insider who had recently been promoted to CEO, announced Organization 2005, a restructuring program that promised to change P&G's culture.

However, not everyone at P&G agreed that such sweeping change was necessary or that the way to achieve it was to reduce investments in the company's core brands in order to fund radical, new products. The organization rebelled, and Jager was forced to resign only 17 months after taking the helm.

The root cause of Jager's very public failure was that he didn't induce P&G employees to cooperate—a requirement of all change campaigns. To achieve such cooperation, managers have a wide variety of tools at their disposal, such as financial incentives, motivational speeches, training programs, and outright threats. But although most competent managers have a good grasp of what cooperation tools are available, we've observed that they may be less sure about which to use. The effectiveness of a given tool depends on the organization's situation. In this article, which employs some ideas from *Do Lunch or Be Lunch,* by Howard Stevenson and Jeffrey Cruikshank, we explain how to choose the right tools and offer advice for managers contemplating change.

Assessing the Existing Level of Agreement

Over our many years observing management successes and failures up close, we've found that the first step in any change initiative must be to assess the level of agreement in the organization along two critical dimensions. The first is the extent to which people agree on *what they want*: the results they seek from their participation in the enterprise; their values and priorities; and which trade-offs they are willing to make in order to achieve those results. Employees at Microsoft, for instance, have historically been united around a common goal: to dominate the desktop. While of course there will always be

pockets of employees who are an exception, this theme
has defined the company's culture. The second dimension is the extent to which people agree on *cause and
effect*: which actions will lead to the desired outcome.
When people have a shared understanding of cause and
effect, they will probably agree about which processes to
adopt—an alignment that was clearly absent at P&G as
Jager attempted to transform the company.

The exhibit "The Agreement Matrix" depicts these
dimensions. The vertical axis shows agreement by an
organization's members on what they want; the horizontal axis shows their agreement on cause and effect.
Employees in organizations in the upper-left quadrant
share hopes for what they will gain from being part of the
organization, even though each might have a different
view of what actions will be required to fulfill those
hopes. Microsoft found itself in this situation in 1995,
when Netscape was threatening to become the primary
"window" through which people would use their computers. Everyone in the company wanted the same
thing—to preserve Microsoft's domination of the desktop—but initially there was little consensus about how
to do that.

Many companies that employ independent contrac-
tors and unionized workers, in contrast, are in the lower-
right corner. These employees may have little passion for
the goals of the company but are willing to follow prescribed procedures if they agree that those actions will
produce the needed results.

In the upper-right quadrant are companies whose
employees agree on what they want *and* how to get
there. Clear consensus on both dimensions makes these
organizations' cultures highly resistant to change: People
are generally satisfied with what they get out of working

in the organization and agree strongly about how to maintain that status quo.

The final scenario is the lower-left quadrant of the agreement matrix, where participants do not agree either on what they want or on how the world works. The perpetually warring nation-states of the Balkan Peninsula exemplify this lack of agreement. We will return to each situation in the following pages.

It's important to note that there is no "best" position for managers to aspire to in the agreement matrix. To

---

The Agreement Matrix

Leaders who want to move their organizations in a new direction must first understand the degree to which employees agree on two dimensions: what they want out of working at the company and cause and effect, or how to achieve what they want. A high level of agreement on both dimensions, such as exists at Apple Computer, requires a completely different set of change tools than leaders will need in, for instance, low-agreement environments.

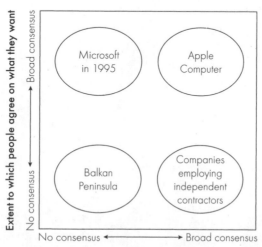

choose the right tools for fostering cooperation among employees, however, managers must assess where their organization lies. The tools that will induce employees in one quadrant to cooperate with a change program may well misfire with employees in a different quadrant. In fact, in any given situation, most tools for eliciting cooperation will not work.

Moving from Agreement to Cooperation

The tools of cooperation can be grouped into four major categories: power, management, leadership, and culture. In the exhibit "The Four Types of Cooperation Tools," we've matched each category with a quadrant of the agreement matrix. While the boundaries are not rigid, the broad labels can give managers a sense of which tools are likely to be effective in various situations.

POWER TOOLS

When members of an organization share little consensus on either dimension of agreement, the only tools that will elicit cooperation are "power tools" such as fiat, force, coercion, and threats. Marshal Josip Broz Tito, the leader of Yugoslavia during most of the Cold War, wielded power tools effectively. He herded the disparate and antagonistic ethnic groups of the Balkan Peninsula into a more or less artificial nation and said, in effect, "I don't care whether you agree with me or with one another about what you want out of life or about how to get it. What I want is for you to look down this gun barrel and cooperate." His approach worked, and the Balkan nations lived in relative peace for several decades.

This is not to suggest, of course, that managers bring firearms to the office. But when organizational factions can't agree on what they want or what to do, power tools are the only ones that work. Jamie Dimon, currently the CEO of JPMorgan Chase, used these tools during the bank's integration with his previous company, Bank One. Convinced that pay had gotten out of control (the head

---

The Four Types of Cooperation Tools

When people in an organization disagree on what they want and on how to achieve desired results, the only tools that induce cooperation are "power tools," which are essentially variations on coercion and fiat. If people want the same thing but disagree on how to achieve it, "leadership tools" such as role modeling and charisma can move them toward a consensus. If people agree strongly on cause and effect but little on what they want, leaders can employ "management tools" such as training and measurement systems. Companies where employees agree on both dimensions of the matrix, and so are generally happy with the status quo, have very strong cultures that are difficult to change. In such circumstances, it is possible only to tweak direction, using such "culture tools" as rituals and folklore. Managers do have other tools at their disposal—such as negotiation and financial incentives—but these will work only when there is a certain level of agreement on both dimensions of the matrix.

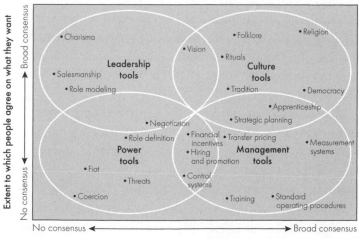

of HR at Bank One was paid more than $5 million), Dimon met with executives individually to tell them they were vastly overpaid and slashed hundreds of salaries by 20% to 50%. He drove a replacement of the firm's myriad IT systems with a single platform, threatening to make all the decisions himself if the IT staff didn't reach any decisions in six weeks. He yanked hundreds of unvisited small-to-midsize businesses from the investment bank's "prospects" list so that the commercial bank could have the chance to work with them. Dimon also reconfigured control systems so that retail branch managers, who had received modest bonuses for meeting sales quotas on mortgages and other products, now stood to lose their jobs for missing quotas.

We have included three tools in the exhibit—negotiation, strategic planning, and financial incentives—to make a point. These tools will work only when there is a modicum of agreement on both dimensions of the matrix. In environments of antagonistic disagreement—whether in the Middle East or in the infamous clashes between Eastern Air Lines' management and its machinist union—negotiation generally doesn't work. A leader might use strategic planning to figure out where the organization ought to go next, but in the absence of the requisite degree of agreement on both dimensions, the strategic plan itself won't elicit the cooperative behavior required to get there.

And using financial incentives—essentially paying employees to want what management wants—may backfire in an environment of low consensus. Consider, for example, the world of K-12 public education, which is decidedly in the lower-left quadrant of the agreement matrix. Teachers, taxpayers, administrators, parents, students, and politicians have divergent priorities and disagree strongly about how to improve. Most pay-for-performance schemes have failed miserably in producing enduring change in schools, because financial incentives are a tool that just won't work in this situation.

Power tools can be extremely effective in low-agreement situations. The key is having the authority to use them. Managers sometimes find themselves in balkanized circumstances without the power to wield the only tools that will induce cooperation under those conditions. If managers are asked to lead a matrixed or "lightweight" project team whose members' loyalties are in conflict with the objectives of the project, for instance, the road to success will be tortuous. Just as a carpenter would never undertake a job without having the requisite tools in his or her toolbox, a wise manager in a low-consensus environment would not agree to lead a change program without the authority to wield the right power tools.

MANAGEMENT TOOLS

The tools of cooperation that drive change in the lower-right quadrant of the agreement matrix focus on coordination and processes. These "management tools" include training, standard operating procedures, and measurement systems. For such tools to work, group members need to agree on cause and effect but not necessarily on what they want from their participation in the organization.

For example, in many companies the reasons unionized manufacturing workers come to work are very different from the reasons senior marketing managers do. But if both groups agree that certain manufacturing procedures will result in products with targeted levels of quality and cost, they will cooperate to follow those procedures.

Measurement systems can also elicit cooperation in such situations. During Intel's first two decades, gross-margin-per-wafer-start was the widely agreed-upon metric for profitability. In the 1980s, the company's DRAM products, which had enjoyed high gross margins in the 1970s, were withering under Japanese competition. Focused on the accepted metric—and even without an explicit executive mandate—middle managers in disparate parts of the organization cooperated to shift manufacturing emphasis from DRAMs to microprocessors, which had become higher-margin products.

LEADERSHIP TOOLS

The tools useful in the upper-left quadrant of the agreement matrix tend to be results oriented rather than process oriented. Such "leadership tools" can elicit cooperation as long as there is a high level of consensus that a change is consistent with the reason employees have chosen to work in the enterprise—even if consensus is low on how to achieve the change. Charismatic leaders respected by employees, for example, often do not address how to get things done. Instead, they motivate people to "just go out and do it." Good sales managers employ these tools skillfully.

Bill Gates used the leadership tool we call vision in his 1995 Internet Tidal Wave memo, which helped Microsoft's employees see that maintaining the company's dominance in the software industry (what they wanted) required an aggressive acknowledgment that the nascent World Wide Web would become an integral part of computing rather than a sideshow to the then-dominant desktop applications—an acknowledgment that ran counter to most employees' deeply held beliefs.

The fierce response of the company's Internet Explorer team crippled Netscape and won Microsoft a more than 90% share of the browser market. Faced with stiff competition from Google in late 2005, Gates reemployed this technique in his memo regarding a "services wave," calling for a shift from sales of shrink-wrapped software to sales of subscriptions.

The same actions viewed as inspiring and visionary among employees in the upper-left corner of the matrix can be regarded with indifference or disdain by those in the lower quadrants. Consider vision statements. When members of a group agree on what they want to achieve, statements that articulate where the organization needs to go can be energizing and inspiring. But if employees don't agree about what they want, vision statements won't help much in changing their behavior—aside from inducing a collective rolling of eyes.

CULTURE TOOLS

In organizations located in the upper-right quadrant of the matrix, employees will cooperate almost automatically to continue in the same direction. Their deep consensus on priorities, and on what set of actions will allow the company to achieve those priorities, is the essence of a strong culture. As MIT's Edgar Schein wrote in *Organizational Culture and Leadership,* culture is "a pattern of shared basic assumptions that was learned by a group as it solved its problems of external adaptation and internal integration, that has worked well enough to be considered valid and, therefore, to be taught to new members as the correct way to perceive, think, and feel in relation to those problems." In organizations with strong cultures, people instinctively prioritize similar options, and their common view of how the world works means that little debate is necessary about the best way to achieve those priorities. Companies with strong cultures in many ways can be self-managing.

But this very strength can make such organizations highly resistant to change. So-called culture tools—such as rituals and folklore—only facilitate cooperation to preserve the status quo; they are not tools of change. Leadership and management tools can also be used in this quadrant to foster cooperation, but only in order to reinforce or enhance the existing culture. A manager of such a company might see herself as a visionary leader wanting to chart a new course for the organization. She may want to use a vision statement as a tool for analyzing and refining the vision in her mind. But as a tool of change? Employees in the upper-right strong-culture quadrant are unlikely to cooperate with any strategy that is at odds with their deeply shared beliefs about what they want and what must be done. Hewlett-Packard's Carly Fiorina learned this the hard way when she tried to challenge the so-called HP Way. Her very public clashes with HP's employees and board led to her ouster in 2005, following the company's controversial merger with Compaq. Essentially, as P&G's Durk Jager needed to recognize, the only tools that can be wielded are those that are effective in the domain *where the employees are*—and in strong cultures, the tools in the upper-right quadrant lead to cooperation in gradual change, at best.

What Managers Can—and Cannot—Do

We noted earlier that there is no "best" position in the matrix of agreement; each quadrant carries its own challenges. A company's position may reflect where it is in its life cycle and is largely determined by how successful it has been. Most organizations start at the left and often at the bottom of the matrix, where the founder's fiats drive much of what gets prioritized and how it gets done. If employees develop effective methods that result in success, consensus will begin to coalesce on the horizontal dimension of agreement—what actions yield the desired results. As the company succeeds, employees who fit with these ways of working, and who want what senior management wants, tend to be promoted. Those who don't tend to leave. Hence, success is the mechanism that builds consensus around what people want and how they can get it. Success shifts the organization toward the upper-right quadrant.

Crisis and failure, in contrast, can destroy that consensus, plunging the organization toward the lower-left quadrant. Employees in crisis are no longer certain or unanimous in their beliefs about what actions are necessary. Managers who are able and willing to use power tools during crises can get employees to cooperate in a remedial course of action, provided those managers know where the organization needs to go and what must be done to get there. Indeed, scholars of organizational change frequently prescribe "creating a crisis" because it forces employees into a situation where they can be compelled to cooperate.

While there is merit to the create-a-crisis strategy, there's a rub to this simple solution: What if the CEO sees the need to change direction while the business is still healthy—when the crisis is in the future, not the present? And what if this healthy company also has an extremely strong culture? That was the situation facing John Sculley, CEO of Apple Computer from 1983 until 1993. Fresh from a triumphant career at PepsiCo, Sculley was an exceptional executive. During his first several years at Apple, the company continued to prosper. By the late 1980s, however, Sculley sensed trouble over the horizon and saw the need to change strategy in three specific ways. First, he saw fledgling low-cost computer makers, such as Dell, menacingly exploring how to make higher-performance computers within their low-cost business models. Sculley declared that Apple needed to move down-market aggressively, reducing its prices by as much as 75% in order to blunt this disruptive attack. Second, before Microsoft introduced its Windows operating system, Sculley urged Apple to open its proprietary product architecture and begin selling its vaunted operating system. Third, he saw that portable, handheld devices would become an important growth market. In retrospect, Sculley saw the future of his industry with remarkable clarity.

But being a visionary leader isn't all it's cracked up to be. When leaders like Sculley conclude that their organization's course must change, they need to consider where the rest of the employees are in the agreement matrix. At Apple, they were decidedly in the upper-right quadrant—some said that Apple put the "cult" in "culture." Sculley tried reorganization, firings, control systems, financial incentives, training, measurement systems, standard procedures, vision statements, salesmanship, strategic planning, and many more tools to elicit cooperation behind the changes he envisioned. But none worked. The Apple employees wouldn't listen.

Sculley gradually lost credibility with his board and employees as tool after tool failed to produce the changes he desired, and he was ousted in 1993. Apple's board then appointed Michael Spindler, head of the company's successful European operations, as CEO. Spindler

also found that the only tools of cooperation at his disposal were those that reinforced Apple's culture, and he
was dismissed after three years. The board then brought
in Gil Amelio, who had turned around the deeply troubled National Semiconductor—expecting that he could
do the same at Apple. He couldn't and was gone in 18
months.

Unable to recruit another qualified CEO, Apple's
board turned in desperation to ousted Apple founder
Steve Jobs as interim CEO. Jobs essentially stopped trying to change the company and instead encouraged the
troops to resume designing cool, innovative, high-end
products such as the iMac and iPod. Apple now domi-
nates the digital music industry. But if there had been
any tools to wield within this strong culture to elicit
cooperation behind the new direction Sculley foresaw,
Apple might have captured much of the fruit that
ultimately fell into the hands of Compaq, Dell, and
Microsoft.

The Tool of Disaggregation

All is not lost for managers who see the need to change a
successful company before the onset of a crisis. They can
wield the tool of *disaggregation*—the separation of organizations into units. This allows managers at the new
unit to build a different consensus among its employees
regarding what they want and how to get there, while the
prior culture continues to thrive in the original unit.

Disaggregation works by eliminating the need for
cooperation between groups with opposing goals. This is
how Hewlett-Packard succeeded in the disruptive ink-jet
printer business even while its laser-jet printer business
was prospering with a very different profit model. HP

disaggregated the printer business, leaving the laser-jet unit in Boise, Idaho, and setting up the ink-jet unit in Vancouver, Washington. Likewise, IBM stayed strong in computers for many years, whereas all its mainframe and minicomputer rivals failed, because it used the tool of disaggregation. When minicomputers began disrupting mainframes, IBM created a separate business unit in Rochester, Minnesota, to focus on minicomputers, which had to be designed, built, and sold within a very different economic model than mainframes. When personal computers disrupted minicomputers, IBM disaggregated again, setting up in Boca Raton, Florida, another free-standing unit, which developed a business model tailored to PCs. Had IBM executives tried to convince the managers and employees of the original computer business to cooperate on a strategy, economic model, and culture to succeed simultaneously in mainframes, minicomputers, and PCs, the company would have failed.

Mastering the Tools of Cooperation at Continental Airlines

It would be rare, of course, for *all* employees in a company to be in one place in the agreement matrix at a given time or across time. While the founding group of senior managers may be in the upper-right quadrant, manufacturing employees may be in the lower-right. Those in sales and creative design might be in the upper-left, sharing an understanding of what is important but unwilling to subject themselves to the sorts of standards and processes that are effective in the lower-right quadrant. Most managers, unfortunately, have a limited tool kit and thus can successfully manage only in certain types of situations. One of the rarest managerial skills is the ability to understand which tools will work in a given situation—and not to waste energy or risk credibility using tools that won't.

Gordon Bethune, CEO of Continental Airlines from 1994 until 2004, was such a manager. Bethune was the airline's tenth CEO in ten years, following a disastrous run including industry worsts in lost baggage, customer complaints, overbooking, and on-time departures. Moreover, Continental had declared bankruptcy twice during the previous decade and was losing $55 million per month despite years of cost cutting.

Bethune turned down the top job twice even though he was already serving as Continental's COO. The first offer was to be acting CEO during the existing CEO's six-month leave of absence, and the second was to serve in the office of the CEO after that executive decided to retire. Although board members respected Bethune, they believed that the only way to restore profitability was through further cost cutting—a path Bethune was convinced would lead to disaster, not deliverance. Given the significant disagreement about how to restore profitability, Bethune knew he could do nothing without the full authority that came with the top job, without the qualifiers of "acting" or "office of."

Even after the board approved Bethune as CEO, few within the company agreed with his unconventional view that Continental needed to be *less* restrictive of its employees and spend *more* in order to get out of bankruptcy. As Bethune wrote in his book *From Worst to First*, when the operations staff rebuffed his instruction to repaint all of the carrier's more than 200 airplanes, he threatened to shoot them unless they complied. Concerned that customer-service employees were micromanaging customers by relying too heavily

on a very thick instruction manual, he set fire to a stack
of manuals in the parking lot.

Having won some initial battles by sheer force,
Bethune achieved preliminary success and began to
move the company out of the lower-left quadrant toward
the upper-right. As the company started to recover,
Bethune began employing more traditional management
tools, including financial incentives. After he offered
each employee a $65 bonus every month that Continen-
tal placed among the top five for on-time departures,
Continental jumped to fourth the subsequent month and
first thereafter. Our model suggests that this incentive
would not have worked in the environment of distrust
and disagreement that characterized the company when
Bethune began his work. By 1998, the company had
posted 11 straight quarters of improved profits and had
won two consecutive J. D. Power and Associates' awards.
Bethune spent the final years of his career using the tools
in the upper-right quadrant, working to reinforce what
has become a very productive culture.

Bethune's well-timed choice of tools mirrored that of
Jack Welch at General Electric, who started out as Neu-
tron Jack, using power tools when the company was a
collection of businesses with vastly different cultures,
operating procedures, and expectations about growth
and profitability. As he oriented the company around the
mantra of being first or second in each of the conglomer-
ate's businesses, GE moved from the lower-left corner of
the matrix toward the upper-right, and Welch shifted his
focus to culture-reinforcing activities, teaching up-and-
coming managers at the company's Crotonville campus.

The success of Bethune and Welch, of course, is both
good news and bad news for their successors. As long as
the shared purposes and unified view of how to achieve
them are appropriate for their companies' challenges,

Larry Kellner and Jeffrey Immelt ought to be able to preside over continued success using the cooperation tools handed to them on their arrival. However, if there are shifts in the competitive environment that mandate significant changes either to what people want or to the required actions, the two CEOs may find that the tools their predecessors used to turn their organizations around cannot be wielded effectively in the strong-culture quadrant.

For example, much has been written about former CEO Lou Gerstner's success in refashioning IBM from a "big iron" company to one built on services. Managing change is always hard. But our model suggests that because he took IBM's helm when the company was in genuine crisis, losing billions of dollars, Gerstner was fortunate. The situation demanded power tools. As IBM's service businesses mature, his successor, Sam Palmisano, may face the tougher challenge. There is no current crisis that enables the effective use of power tools to marshal a cooperative march in a new direction. He faces a cultural challenge that will likely prove more difficult than the crisis Gerstner faced.

Bethune, Welch, and Gerstner were blessed with an instinct for choosing the right tools at the right time. Our hope is that by making the instincts of effective managers more explicit, even those of us who are not born knowing how to manage change can learn to do so more effectively.

The Tools of Politics

IN INSTITUTIONS with well-established cultures (those in the upper-right portion of the exhibit "The Agreement

Matrix"), democracy can be used as a tool to encourage cooperation. An important insight from this model is that democracy will not work except where people agree strongly on both dimensions of the matrix: what they want and the rules of cause and effect. The very functioning of democracy depends upon the existence of strong cultural beliefs that are often rooted in the teachings of certain religions. The religious institutions at the root of these cultures have taught that people are meant to be free and that they should voluntarily be honest and respect the life, property, and equal opportunity of others—because even if the police don't catch and punish them, they will be rewarded or punished in some way in the afterlife. The successful practice of these beliefs—together with a shared value that every person should be allowed to worship God in his or her own way—has created successful societies in places such as India, Japan, the United States, and Western Europe. The practices have become so deeply embedded over so many years that almost all people in these societies, regardless of religious belief, now strongly share these values and are ensconced in the upper-right quadrant of the agreement matrix. The vast majority of people living in these cultures obey the law voluntarily—and, as a result, democracy works.

On occasion, Americans in particular have tried to impose democracy on countries whose populations are not in the upper-right corner of the agreement matrix— where religious or other institutions have not built the type of cultural consensus that is consistent with democratic principles. When America has essentially snapped its fingers at these countries, ordering them to establish stable democracies—and quickly—chaos typically has ensued. The crime, corruption, and tax evasion that characterize much of Russia; the collapse of civil order that torments Haiti; and the costly, tragic dilemma that America now faces in Iraq—all are testaments to the fact that democracy doesn't work when the enabling preconditions don't exist.

Originally published in October 2006
Reprint R0610D

About the Contributors

JEFF BEZOS is the founder and CEO of Amazon.com.

JOSEPH L. BOWER is the Donald K. David Professor of Business Administration at Harvard Business School in Boston.

CLAYTON M. CHRISTENSEN is the Robert and Jane Cizik Professor of Business Administration at Harvard Business School in Boston.

CLARK G. GILBERT is an administrator at Brigham Young University, Idaho, in Rexburg, and a former Harvard Business School professor.

PAUL HEMP is a senior editor at *Harvard Business Review*.

JEFFREY R. IMMELT is the chairman and CEO of General Electric.

JULIA KIRBY is the editor, Special Issues, at *Harvard Business Review*.

MICHAEL C. MANKINS is a partner in the San Francisco office of Bain & Company, a global management consulting firm.

MATT MARX is a doctoral student at Harvard Business School.

ANITA M. MCGAHAN is the Everett V. Lord Distinguished Faculty Scholar and professor at Boston University's School of Management and a senior institute associate at the Institute for Strategy and Competitiveness at Harvard University in Cambridge.

SAMUEL J. PALMISANO is the CEO of IBM.

RICHARD STEELE is a partner in the New York office of Marakon Associates, a strategy and management consulting firm.

HOWARD H. STEVENSON is the Sarofim-Rock Professor of Business Administration at Harvard Business School and the vice provost for Harvard University Resources and Planning. He is also the chairman of the board for Harvard Business School Publishing.

THOMAS A. STEWART is the editor and managing director of *Harvard Business Review*.

CHRIS ZOOK is the author of *Unstoppable: Finding Hidden Assets to Renew the Core and Fuel Profitable Growth* and leads the Global Strategy Practice of Bain & Company.

Index